STALAG LUFT III

IMAGES OF WAR

STALAG LUFT III

THE GERMAN POW CAMP THAT INSPIRED *THE GREAT ESCAPE*

RARE PHOTOGRAPHS FROM WARTIME ARCHIVES

Charles Messenger

Greenhill Books

First published in Great Britain in 2019 by

Greenhill Books

c/o Pen & Sword Books Ltd, 47 Church Street, Barnsley,
South Yorkshire, S70 2AS, England
For more information on our books, please visit
www.greenhillbooks.com, email contact@greenhillbooks.com
or write to us at the above address.

Charles Messenger text © Greenhill Books, 2019
Peter Wilkinson maps © Greenhill Books, 2019

ISBN 978-1-78438-446-3

The right of Charles Messenger to be identified as author of this work has been asserted by him in accordance with Section 77 of the Copyright, Designs and Patents Act 1988.

A CIP catalogue record for this book is available from the British Library.

All rights reserved. No part of this book may be reproduced or transmitted in any form or by any means, electronic or mechanical including photocopying, recording or by any information storage and retrieval system, without permission from the Publisher in writing.

Typeset by Concept, Huddersfield, West Yorkshire, HD4 5JL.
Printed and bound in India by Replika Press Pvt. Ltd

Contents

Acknowledgements 6

Introduction 7

Other Sources on Stalag Luft III 13

Chapter One
   The Camp 15

Chapter Two
   The Germans 27

Chapter Three
   External Agencies and Prisoner Welfare 35

Chapter Four
   Daily Life 43

Chapter Five
   Prisoner Personalities 69

Chapter Six
   The Intelligence War 79

Chapter Seven
   Escaping 87

Chapter Eight
   Two Famous Escapes 99

Chapter Nine
   Great Escape Aftermath 119

Chapter Ten
   The Camp Today 137

Acknowledgements

The author is most grateful to the following for their help: Michael Codner (nephew of Michael Codner of Wooden Horse fame), Luka Cyrian, Marek Lazarz (Curator, the POW Camps Museum), Robert J. Laplander, Simon Pearson, Dr Mary Rowell (Chief of Special Collections, McDermott Library, US Air Force Academy), and Jon Wilkinson.

Introduction

Stalag Luft III and Colditz are the best known of the German prisoner-of-war camps of the Second World War. Both have been the subject of numerous books and Colditz triggered two British television series (in 1972–74 and 2005) and the film *The Colditz Story* (1955). Stalag Luft III, however, was the subject of what is perhaps one of Hollywood's best-known feature films, *The Great Escape* (1963), starring, among others, Steve McQueen and Richard Attenborough. It told the story of the camp's main claim to fame, or perhaps notoriety: the mass escape of seventy-six Allied air force officers through a tunnel in March 1944, fifty of whom were later shot by the Gestapo on the orders of Adolf Hitler. This was by no means the only escape from the camp, which housed British, Dominion and American airmen, as well as many from the countries of Nazi-occupied Europe and even captured Soviet officers.

During most of the war, from 1939 to 1945, the German POW camp system was run on individual service lines. Thus the German Navy had its own camps for captured sailors (Marine-Lager or Marlag for short), while the Army had Stammlager (Stalag – 'permanent camps') for other ranks and Offizier-lager (Oflag) for officers. The Luftwaffe's camps were termed Stalag Luft. Generally, although it was by no means a cast-iron rule, captured Allied soldiers were first processed through a Durchgangslager (Dulag or 'transit camp'). The Luftwaffe equivalent was the Dulag Luft and it was here that downed aircrew were interrogated prior to being sent to a Stalag Luft. The main Dulag Luft, through which most of the inmates of Stalag Luft III passed, was at Oberursel, just north of Frankfurt am Main. This received its first prisoners in December 1939 and initially was the sole Luftwaffe camp until Stalag Luft I was opened in July 1940 at Barth in Pomerania, on the Baltic coast. As more and more Allied aircrew were captured, especially as a result of the ever-increasing bomber offensive against Germany, so other Luftwaffe camps were built.

What was to become Stalag Luft III itself originated in an order from Hermann Goering, Commander-in-Chief of the Luftwaffe, for the construction of a new air force officers' camp near the small town of Sagan (now Żagan), which lies in the north-east corner of what was then German Silesia and virtually midway between Berlin and Breslau (today Wrocław). Indeed, Sagan was an important rail junction, being the meeting point of no fewer than six railway lines. The station itself was also less than a mile from the site of the new POW camp, which was tempting for POWs bent on escape. The camp was sited in a wooded area, but more significant was that the camp was built on soil containing much sand of a distinctive yellow colour. It was also adjacent to Stalag VIIIC, which contained Polish and Russian prisoners in very poor conditions. The Germans were well aware, from their experiences at Oberursel and Barth, that the British POWs in particular were very keen on tunnelling as a means of escape, and reckoned that the sand would make tunnel construction more difficult because of the increased danger of tunnel collapse, as well as making it easier to detect a tunnel that was being dug. This would not deter the inmates, however. Indeed, some 100 tunnels would be constructed in the camp, although the vast majority were detected before they could be used.

The first prisoners entered what became known as the camp's East Compound in April 1942. They came from Oberursel, Barth and Oflag VIB at Warburg. By the end of the month the East Compound had 385 inmates. Among them were a number of intrepid escapers. At the same time, the adjacent Centre Compound was opened for non-commissioned aircrew, with 200 arriving from Stalag Luft I that same April. Further batches of NCOs were sent from other camps until by late autumn 1942 the Centre Compound housed some 1,800 POWs, while the East Compound contained approximately 700 officer POWs. The vast majority were members of the RAF and Dominion forces, but there were also naval pilots from the Fleet Air Arm and one or two army officers who had somehow slipped through the net. Wearing RAF uniform were three Americans, members of the Eagle squadrons, which were made up of Americans who had volunteered to fight for Britain before the USA entered the war. In September 1942 the first members of the US Army Air Force arrived, some shot down over France and Belgium and others over North Africa, where US air power was beginning to lend its weight. American numbers soon began to increase and in November 1942 the camp authorities decided to segregate them in their own hut in the East Compound.

Even though further Luftwaffe camps were opening, there was a constant stream of new inmates for Stalag Luft III and work began on a new compound. The construction was largely carried out by Russian POWs and what became the North Compound opened for business at the end of March 1943, with 850 POWs being transferred from the East Compound. They included several key members of the escape organisation. Almost as soon as they had moved, work began on three tunnels, known as Tom, Dick and Harry. This did not, however, mean a cessation of escape efforts in the East Compound. Indeed, in July–October 1943 a tunnel was dug under the wire and in what became known as the Wooden Horse escape, the three officers taking part making a successful 'home run' to neutral Sweden. That summer, most of the NCOs left the Centre Compound for Stalag Luft VI, which was situated in present-day Lithuania. Their place was taken by newly arrived Americans. Those Americans already in the camp were moved to the recently constructed South Compound in October 1943. The numbers of new arrivals were indicative of the heavy losses that the US Eighth Army Air Force was suffering in its daylight bombing offensive against Germany, and also the extraction of American POWs from Italy after that country's September 1943 armistice with the Allies. One further expansion of Stalag Luft III took place in January 1944. A satellite camp had been built at Belaria, some 3 miles (5km) west of Sagan, and 500 RAF officers from the Centre and East Compounds were initially sent there to make more room. Further prisoners were sent from the North Compound in March and later in the year others, including Americans, arrived from Oberursel, giving an ultimate total of some 1,200 inmates. The final compound to be opened was West Compound in April 1944. It was the largest of the compounds, with 17 barrack huts, and housed Americans.

The aftermath of the Great Escape in March 1944 brought about a significant change of mood among the 'Kriegies' (short for *Kriegsgefangene* – prisoners of war), as the American POWs in German hands called themselves. The realisation that so many of those who got out through the tunnel had been shot in cold blood by the Gestapo acted as a deterrent to escape attempts, as did warning notices posted in the camps by the Germans that escaping would no longer be considered by them a game. The Normandy landings in June 1944 and the spectacular Soviet advances on the Eastern Front also made it clear that the tide had turned irreversibly against the Germans and the final defeat of the Nazis was only a matter of time. Indeed, the British issued a formal order to their officer POWs that escape was no longer to be encouraged. As 1944 wore on, the Stalag Luft III inmates became increasingly concerned that the Germans might massacre them. To counter this, the compounds covertly organised themselves into military units and stockpiled makeshift weapons. However, in early January 1945 the Russians launched a major offensive across the River Vistula. It soon became clear to the prisoners that the Germans intended to evacuate the camp and march them westwards to avoid them falling into Soviet hands. The POWs made some preparation for this and it was just as well. On 27 January, with less than an hour's warning, they were marched out, compound by compound. It was the end of Stalag Luft III.

Stalag Luft III lay roughly midway between Berlin and Breslau (Wrocław).

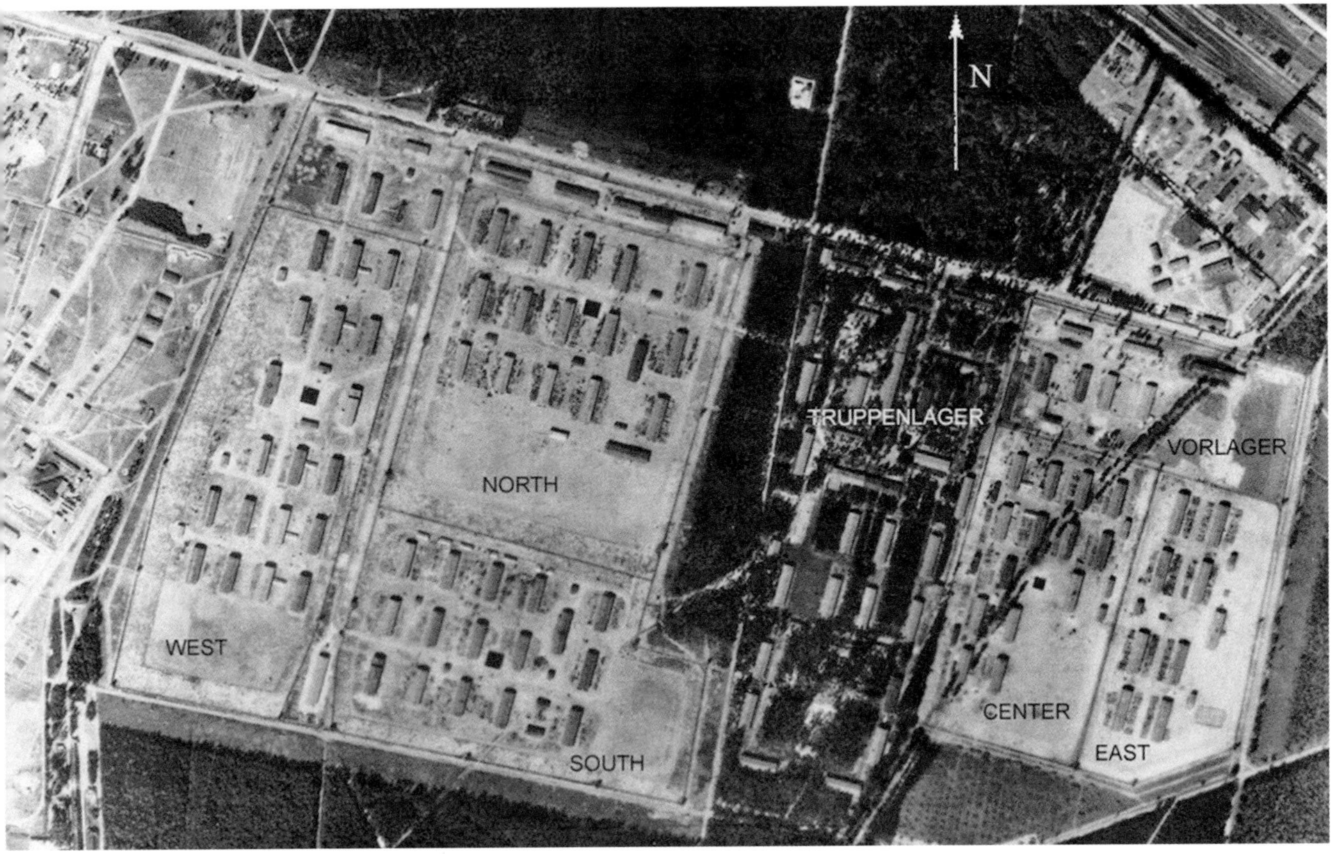

US Army Air Force photograph of Stalag Luft III in its finished state. The *Truppenlager* was more commonly known as the *Kommandantur* and the camp to the west of the West Compound is Stalag VIIIC. *(USAAF)*

A typical Stalag Luft III scene. Looking across the south-west corner of the North Compound into the West Compound, as viewed from the South Compound. *(USAFA, SMS 329)*

Other Sources on Stalag Luft III

Stalag Luft III: The Official History of the 'Great Escape' POW Camp, Barnsley: Frontline Books, 2016

Carroll, Tim, *The Great Escape from Stalag Luft III: The Full Story of How 76 Allied Officers Carried Out World War II's Most Remarkable Mass Escape*, New York: Pocket Books, pb. edn, 2004

Clark, Albert C., *33 Months as a POW in Stalag Luft III: A World War II Airman Tells His Story*, Golden CA: Fulcrum Publishing, 2004

Davies, Stephen R., *A Global History of the RAF Police*, Volume 5: *The Great Escape Stalag Luft III*, published privately (no date)

Durand, Arthur A., *Stalag Luft III: The Secret Story*, Wellingborough: Patrick Stephens, 1989

James, B. A. 'Jimmy', *Moonless Night: The Second World War Escape Epic*, Barnsley: Pen & Sword, 2018

Laplander, Robert J., *The True Story of the Wooden Horse*, Barnsley: Pen & Sword, 2014

Müller, Jens, *The Great Escape from Stalag Luft III*, London: Greenhill Books, 2019

Pearson, Simon, *The Great Escaper: The Life and Death of Roger Bushell – Love, Betrayal, Big X and the Great Escape*, London: Hodder & Stoughton, pb. edn, 2014

Rees, Wing Commander Ken, with Arrandale, Karen, *Lie in the Dark and Listen: The Remarkable Exploits of a WWII Bomber Pilot and Great Escaper*, London: Grub Street, pb edn, 2017

Vance, Jonathan, *The True Story of the Great Escape*, London: Greenhill Books, 2019

Vanderstok, Bram, *Escape from Stalag Luft III: The True Story of my Successful Great Escape*, Barnsley: Greenhill Books, 2019

Walton, Marilyn Jeffers and Eberhardt, Michael C., *From Commandant to Captive: The Memoirs of Stalag Luft III Commandant Col. Friedrich Wilhelm von Lindeiner von Waldau with Postwar Interviews, Letters, and Testimony*, Lulu Publishing Services, 2015

Williams, Eric, *The Wooden Horse*, Barnsley: Pen & Sword, 2013 edn

Chapter One

The Camp

In its final state, Stalag Luft III comprised a number of self-contained compounds. One was the Kommandantur, which held the camp staff and guards. The five POW compounds were of varying sizes, with the North Compound being the largest in terms of space, especially on account of its large sports field. The Germans had planned to use part of the field for extra huts, but this never came to fruition. The North, South and West Compounds shared what the Germans called a *Vorlager*. There is no direct English translation for this word, but 'outer camp' approximates to its meaning. It consisted of the sick bay, coal stores, a mail room and the cells, besides two guard rooms. Both the Centre and East Compounds were served by another *Vorlager*.

Each compound was surrounded by two 9ft-tall barbed wire fences, made up of vertical and horizontal rows of barbed wire. They had inward facing overhangs to make it more difficult to get over them and were 7ft apart. Rolls of barbed wire lay on the ground between them as a further escape deterrent. Approximately 30ft from the inner fence was a cable 2ft off the ground. Any prisoner crossing this line was liable to be shot. Prisoners were, however, allowed to retrieve balls which had gone over it, provided they alerted the guards beforehand. Overlooking the compounds were a series of guard towers, which were manned by day and night. They were some 150yds apart and were equipped with rifles, semi-automatic weapons and machine guns. At night they used searchlights to sweep the area.

The compounds consisted of a number of barrack huts, a cook house, a bath house, latrines and a theatre, which was constructed by the prisoners. The barrack huts were raised off the ground and supported on a number of concrete piles. This was to dissuade the POWs from tunnelling under the huts. The huts had a number of living rooms each capable of holding six to fourteen men, a wash room, a night latrine and a kitchen. There were also a couple of small rooms for senior officers.

The main street of Stalag VIIIC, Stalag Luft III's next-door neighbour.
(USAFA, SMS 329)

The main gate of the South Compound.
(USAFA, SMS 329)

General view of the North Compound. Note the low warning fence beyond which the prisoners were forbidden to go. Walking the perimeter was a standard form of exercise and was one way of enabling confidential conversations, especially on escape matters. (*Australian War Memorial*)

Another view of the camp, showing how close the woods were to it. Indeed, new compounds could only be built by cutting down trees. (*USAFA, SMS 329*)

A winter scene. *(USAFA, SMS 329)*

A typical watchtower, known as Goon Boxes by the prisoners. *(USAFA, SMS 329)*

When the camp looked likely to run out of room, tents had to be erected, as is being done here by Russians POWs. *(USAFA, SMS 329)*

The end result. *(USAFA, SMS 329)*

A compound cookhouse, showing the boilers in which most of the German ration food was cooked. The boilers were also the main source of hot water. *(USAFA, SMS 329)*

The South Compound's theatre. This was constructed by the POWs themselves, with the seats being made from Red Cross parcel boxes. *(USAFA, SMS 329)*

The South Compound's incinerator and empty can bank. The Germans recycled the cans, although the prisoners often found other uses for them. *(USAFA, SMS 329)*

A typical barrack hut layout as drawn by an American POW. *(USAFA)*

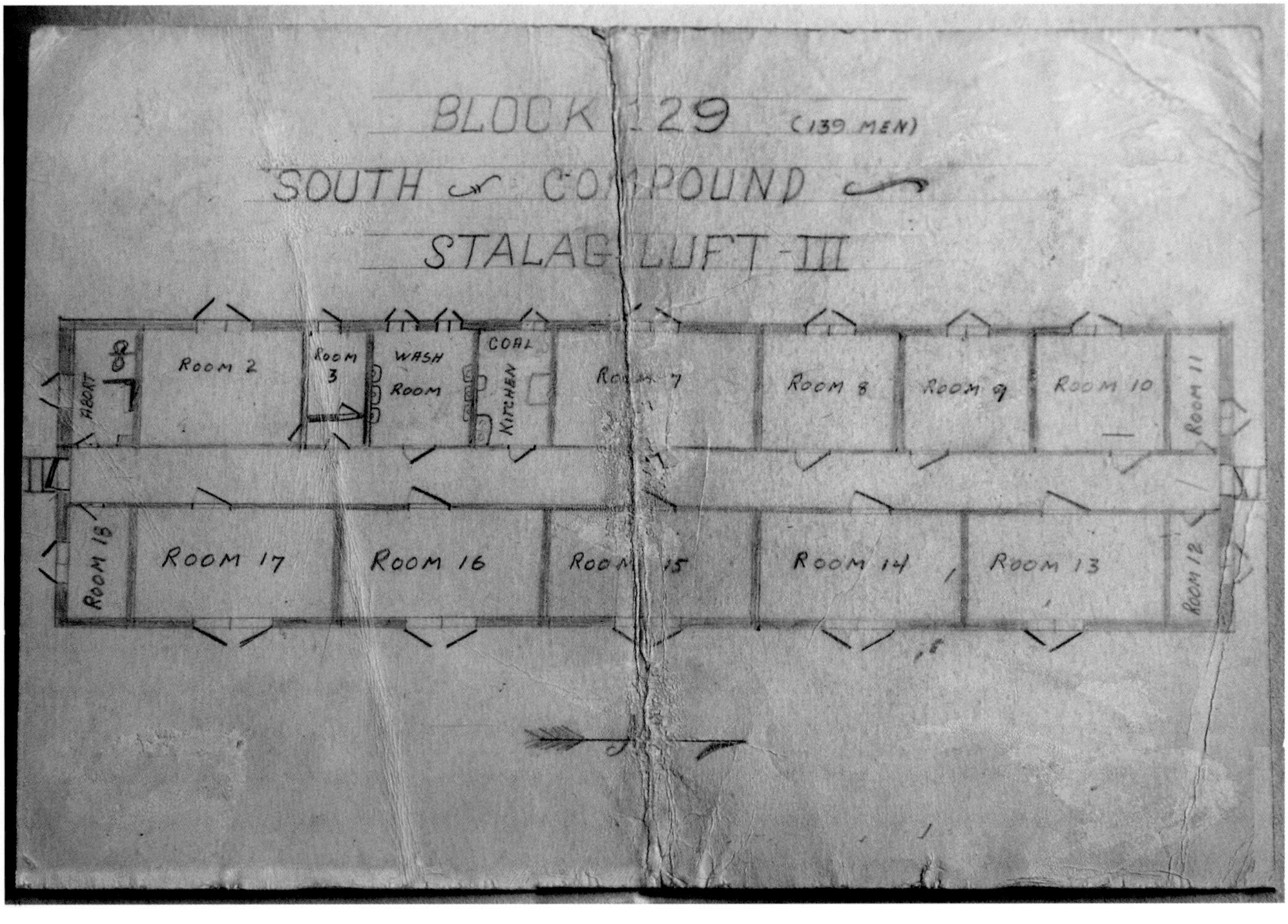

A barrack room, showing how cluttered it could become. Apart from the bunk beds, much of the furniture was made by the prisoners themselves. *(USAFA, SMS 329)*

A typical barrack room stove. It was very inefficient, not helped by the very low quality of what coal the Germans were able to provide. *(USAFA, SMS 329)*

A washroom. Only cold water was provided. (USAFA, SMS 329)

Contents of a barrack room cupboard. Much of it was cans of Red Cross food. (USAFA, SMS 329)

Barrack wash room.
(USAFA, SMS 329)

There was little privacy in the latrines.
(USAFA, SMS 329)

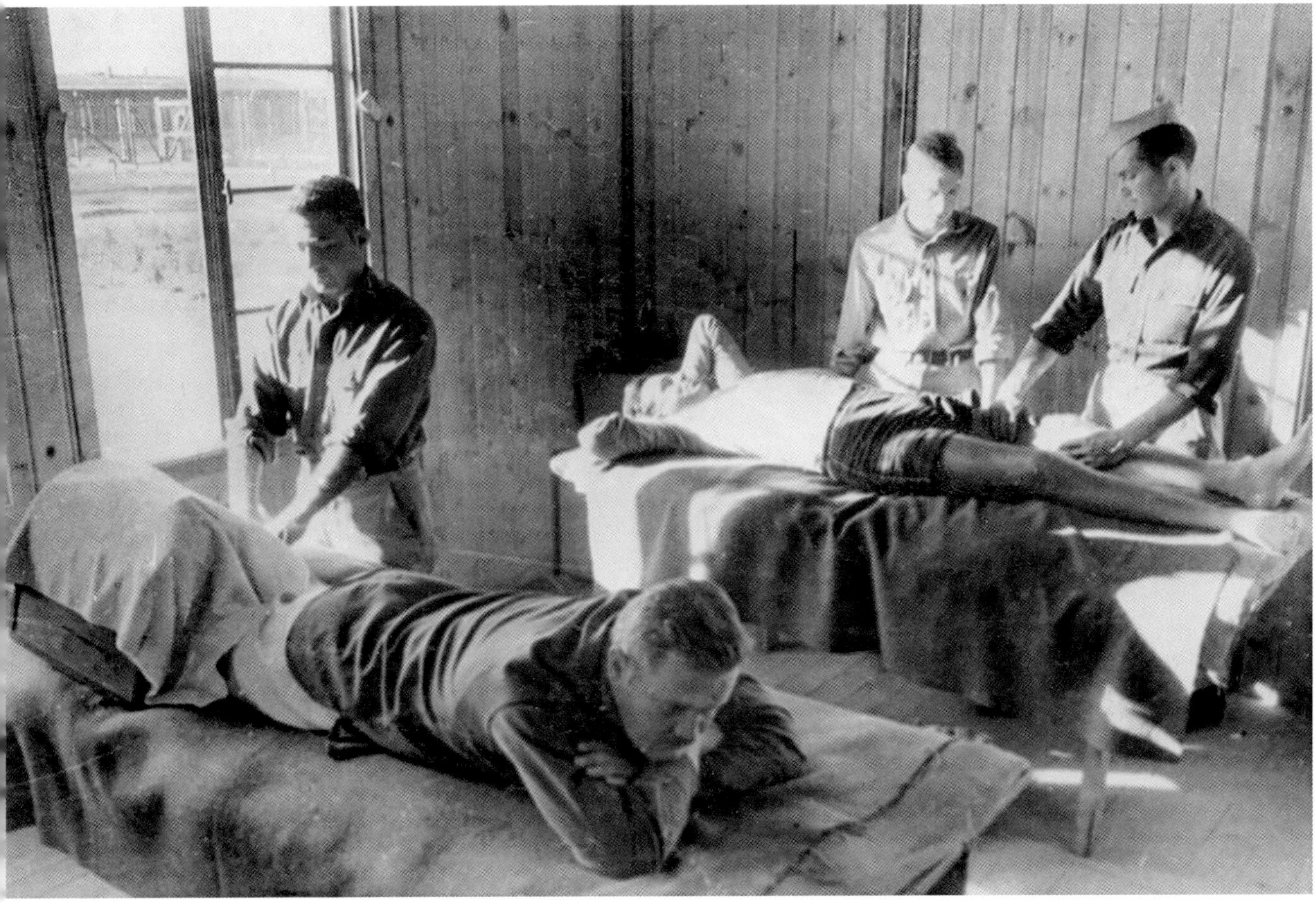

The physiotherapy room in the medical centre, which was situated in the Vorlager outside the POW compounds. (*USAFA, SMS 329*)

Each barrack hut had two lavatories, for 150–200 men. They were used only at night, with the compound communal latrines available by day. (*USAFA, SMS 329*)

As fire precautions each hut had a tub full of water and one fire extinguisher. (*USAFA, SMS 329*)

Chapter Two

The Germans

For most of the war the German POW camp system was under the ultimate control of the *Oberkommando der Wehrmacht* (OKW – Armed Forces Supreme Headquarters). Beneath this, camps were the responsibility of the single service headquarters, with the *Oberkommando der Luftwaffe* (OKL) having charge of all air force camps. The Luftwaffe had an inspector-general of POW camps, but the camps themselves came directly under the local Luftwaffe District (*Gau*) headquarters. In the case of Stalag Luft III, this was *Luftgau 3*, and later *Luftgau 13*.

The Commandant of Stalag Luft III for much of the war was, to give him his full name, *Oberst* Friedrich Wilhelm von Lindeiner genannt von Wildau. He took command shortly after the camp opened and remained in charge until he was sacked in the immediate aftermath of the March 1944 Great Escape. Von Lindeiner was a typical member of the Prussian aristocracy. Commissioned into the Guards in 1898, he was seconded to the German colonial forces in East Africa four years later. He returned to the Prussian Army in 1908 and fought with distinction during the First World War, being twice seriously wounded. After the war, von Lindeiner left the army and went into business, settling in Holland (he had married a Dutch aristocrat in 1909). In 1932 he returned to Germany but eventually had to end his business activities in 1937 because of difficulties with the Nazis. Instead, he joined Hermann Goering's personal staff as a civilian. Although he wanted to retire, in 1940 he was reactivated and worked in Western Armies intelligence. Eventually, he found himself in charge of Stalag Luft III.

Colonel von Lindeiner was, by all accounts, very correct in his dealings with the POWs. He spoke fluent English and did his best to observe the Geneva Convention, although he often felt that his superiors were not giving him the necessary backing. He also faced increasing problems with the Gestapo, since Heinrich Himmler, overall head of the SS, wanted to take control of all POW camps as part of his 'empire building'. Von Lindeiner did, however, have a temper and was especially exasperated by the prisoners when he felt that they were not conducting themselves as officers should. On the other hand, he delegated the day-to-day running of the camp to the prisoners as much as he could. He was, nonetheless, constantly pressured by the compounds' Senior Allied Officers over strict observance of the Geneva Convention.

The administration of the camp was split into seven departments. The first was the *Kommandantur* (headquarters). This was where von Lindeiner himself worked, with his adjutant and the legal officer. Department II was responsible for camp administration and was headed by the camp's second-in-command, Major Gustav Simoleit. In civilian life he was an academic, with a gift for languages, especially Russian and Eastern European languages, and was responsible for the day-to-day running of the compounds. He was generally liked by the prisoners. Under Simoleit each compound had two officers, the equivalent of a warrant officer, and five NCOs allotted to it. They all spoke English and many were, in fact, Austrian and some were not especially well disposed to Nazi Germany. In addition, Department II was responsible for maintaining a card index system with the personal details of each POW. Simoleit also had a detachment of Russian POWs under his command. This detachment was responsible for maintaining the camp's transport (both motor and horse-drawn) and the electricity plant, and taking care of the camp's pigs and chickens, as well as its vegetable garden. These helped to supplement the basic rations.

Department III covered counter-intelligence. This came under the *Abwehr* (German military intelligence) and had a separate chain of command. Until May 1943 it was headed by Major Peschel and then, until after the Great Escape, by Captain Frans Brioli. The basic role of the POW branch of the *Abwehr* was to guard against acts of sabotage and espionage in the German Reich. In practice, this mainly came down to a ceaseless battle to detect POW escape attempts before they happened. The principal method involved small teams of four or five specially trained men, known as Ferrets, under an NCO, one to each compound, who spent their days inside the camp in an attempt to discover preparations for escape. *Oberfeldwebel* (Warrant Officer) Hermann Glemnitz, the chief Ferret, was one of the camp characters. Born in 1898, he was called up for military service in 1916 as an infantryman, but transferred to the flying service and had just completed his pilot training when the war ended. Between the wars Glemnitz had jobs in many parts of the world, and learnt English, Spanish and French. Conscripted again in 1939, he fought in Poland and France as a Luftwaffe anti-aircraft gunner. He then fell sick and was assigned to Stalag Luft I as an interpreter. From there he moved to Stalag Luft III when British POWs were first transferred there and eventually became the chief Ferret. Glemnitz was highly respected by the prisoners for his shrewdness and total incorruptibility.

The fourth branch covered logistics and handled food, including Red Cross parcels, as well as clothing and other stores. Department V was responsible for all medical aspects. Initially, the camp had just one *Revier* (sick bay) with forty beds and a dental unit. It was overseen by a German doctor, with two British doctors attending to the patients. A French-run hospital, a mile from the camp, carried out operations and the local hospital in Sagan performed X-rays. As the camp expanded, so did the medical facilities, but they were never sufficient. Lack of medicines, too, was a problem, with much reliance being placed on what the Red Cross produced. What is remarkable is the infrequency of epidemics, which could have posed a very real problem, given the numbers of men living cheek by jowl with one another.

Censorship was carried out by Department VI under Captain Guenther von Massow, the brother of a Luftwaffe general. He had run the censorship department at Oberursel and was well known to some of the early POWs at Stalag Luft III. Under him von Massow had some 30 male and 180 female translators by the end of the camp's existence. The latter were housed in separate barracks and, for obvious reasons, were not permitted in the compounds. The translators dealt with both incoming and outgoing mail and, as far as possible, each checked the correspondence of a particular group of POWs; familiarity with their thinking and phraseology meant they were more likely to be able to detect unusual messages, which might be coded. Because of the strain induced by trying to read illegible writing, their working hours were restricted to seven hours a day.

Department VII looked after the guards, whose overall total appears to have been fixed at approximately 10 per cent of the POW strength. They were organised in 150-man companies. Most were classed in a lower medical category through age or wounds, or were very young. They were rotated fairly frequently. They were faced with the threat of being sent to the Eastern Front if they failed in their duty. They were called Goons by the prisoners after some primitive and rather stupid characters featured in a British *Daily Mirror* cartoon strip.

One other sub-unit, the camp construction staff, should also be mentioned. This was the responsibility of a Reserve officer who was a local businessman. Initially, he was given two detachments of Jewish slave workers, but there was general disgust at their pitiful conditions and they were replaced by POWs of various nationalities.

(**Opposite, above**) A Luftwaffe general visiting the North Compound. Group Captain Martin Massey is on his right and Major Simoleit, Deputy Camp Commandant, on his left. (USAFA, SMS 329)

(**Above**) Colonel Friedrich von Lindeiner, Commandant of Stalag Luft III, May 1942 to March 1944. He was always correct in his dealing with the POWs and they generally respected him. (USAFA, SMS 329)

(**Opposite, below**) Major Gustav Simoleit in his office. He remained in post throughout almost all of the camp's existence and was with some of its inmates until the very end of the war. (USAFA, SMS 329)

Simoleit took a deep interest in the prisoners' activities and the Americans, in particular, regarded him almost as a friend. *(USAFA, SMS 329)*

Hermann Glemnitz, the Chief Ferret. Like Simoleit, he remained with the POWs until the bitter end. Respected for his efficiency and sense of duty, he also had a genuine sense of humour. *(USAFA, SMS 329)*

American POWs talking to two Ferrets, recognisable by their overalls. The Ferrets fought a ceaseless battle to discover preparations for escapes. (USAFA, SMS 329)

American prisoners talking to two Lager officers. They tended to be more friendly to the Germans than the British, who often tried to rile the guards and the Ferrets, believing this to be another dimension to the war against Nazi Germany. *(USAFA, SMS 329)*

Chapter Three

External Agencies and Prisoner Welfare

The treatment of prisoners of war was bound by the Geneva Convention of 1929. This itself was based on the Hague Conventions of 1899 and 1907, but revised to reflect the experience of the First World War. After defining what a prisoner of war was, the Convention went on to lay down how they should be treated on capture, stressing that POWs must be evacuated away from the combat zone as soon as possible, but they were not allowed to be marched more than 12½ miles (20km) per day on their feet. When it came to prisoner questioning, they did not have to tell their captors more than their rank, name and number. POW camps had to have equivalent facilities to those that the detaining power provided in its own base installations. Food had to be of the same quality as that of the detaining power's troops at the base. Interestingly, the Convention laid down that prisoners of different race or nationality should not be in the same camp. This was the reason why the Americans at Stalag Luft III, once they were present in sufficient numbers, were segregated from the RAF POWs. There had to be adequate medical facilities and the POWs had to be allowed to follow their religious observances. POW camps should also provide recreational facilities, both sporting and intellectual. Officers were not permitted to work, while other ranks had to be given labour that was unconnected to the war effort. There is no doubt that the Germans generally observed the Geneva Convention when it came to Western Allied prisoners, although this was less so during the latter stages of the war. The same was not the case with the millions of Russian prisoners who fell into German hands, as the Nazis regarded the Slav race as *Untermenschen* (sub-humans). Besides which, the Soviet Union had not ratified the Geneva Convention. Thus the Third Reich felt justified in treating Russian POWs with the utmost brutality.

To ensure that the Convention was observed, it laid down that when two countries had broken off diplomatic relations with each other, a neutral state would be appointed as the Protecting Power to act as a diplomatic conduit between the warring nations and look after the interests of their respective citizens who found themselves beleaguered in a hostile country. This also included prisoners of war.

During the Second World War both Britain and the USA used Switzerland as the Protecting Power, as did the Germans. Complaints about the treatment of their respective POWs would be passed through the Swiss government, which also carried out inspections of camps to ensure that the Geneva Convention was being observed. In Germany this was done by members of the Swiss legation to Berlin.

Two other agencies were also directly involved in ensuring the well-being of the POWs. The first was the International Commission of the Red Cross (ICRC). One important aspect of its work was a tracing service to locate the whereabouts of POWs to enable their families to get in touch with them. It was through the Commission that the parents of Roger Bushell, who became the mastermind of the Great Escape from Stalag Luft III, learnt that he was a POW at Oberursel. The ICRC also fulfilled five other important functions. The first was to provide medical support for the POWs. This took the form of medical parcels containing medicines, bandages and information booklets. Red Cross representatives also provided advice when visiting the camps. Most important were the food parcels, which were issued at the rate of one parcel per POW per week. Most parcels were distributed by national branches of the Red Cross and the contents differed from country to country. Thus, the early American arrivals at Stalag Luft III did not think very much of the British Red Cross parcels, which they were forced to make use of until the US Red Cross had set up its own distribution system. The parcels played a major part in sustaining the POWs, especially given the poor quality of the German issue rations. National Red Cross organisations also provided clothing for the POWs, although again it was not until the autumn of 1943 that the American Red Cross was in a position to supply this. Finally, the Red Cross supplied reading material for the POWs, with the camps, especially Stalag Luft III, building up extensive libraries. Families, too, were allowed to send their loved ones parcels containing food, clothing, books and games, the ration being one parcel every two months. There were other domestic charities which did the same.

In addition to the Red Cross, there was the Young Men's Christian Association (YMCA). During the First World War this gave aid to both Allied and German POWs. Early in the Second World War the International YMCA Aid for Prisoners of War was re-established. It was the Swedish YMCA which took the lead in looking after the camps in Germany and German-occupied Poland. The principal task was supplying reactional materials – musical instruments, sports equipment, theatrical costumes and equipment, gramophones and records, films, toilet articles, as well as books – to the POWs. As far as Stalag Luft III was concerned, one YMCA figure stood out. This was Henry Soderberg, a young, newly qualified Swedish lawyer, who volunteered to work with POW Aid and arrived in Berlin in April 1943. He soon made a deep impression on the camps he looked after in eastern Germany and German-occupied Poland, especially Stalag Luft III. Driven out of Berlin in August

1943 by the bombing, Soderberg established his office and YMCA store in Sagan, thus placing himself on the camp's doorstep. He made a number of close friends, especially in the Americans' compounds, and kept in touch with them after the war, even attending some of their reunions in the USA.

US officers on a parole stroll with a member of the Swiss Embassy in Berlin, the Protecting Power. *(USAFA, SMS 329)*

The Senior British Officer meets Red Cross representatives at the main gate of his compound. (USAFA, SMS 329)

AN AMERICAN RED CROSS STANDARD FOOD PARCEL

FEBRUARY – 1944

---

1 6-oz. carton of Type K-2 biscuit
1 8-oz. carton of processed American cheese
4 2-oz. bars of chocolate
1 2-oz. tin of soluble coffee
1 12-oz. tin of corned beef
1 16-oz. carton of dried prunes
1 6-oz. tin of liver paste
1 16-oz. tin of whole powdered milk
1 16-oz. tin of Vitamin A fortified oleomargarine
1 6-oz. tin of Jam
1 12-oz. tin of pork luncheon meat
1 7-3/4-oz. tin of salmon
1 8-oz. carton of white lump sugar
5 pkgs. containing 100 cigarettes
2 2-oz. bars of odorless soap
1 pkg. ascorbic acid tablets (Vitamin C)

An American Red Cross parcel. This provided each POW with an additional 900 calories per day, if he received a parcel each week. The German rations represented a daily 1,500—1,900 calories, but a reasonably active male needs some 3,000 calories per day to sustain him. Thus the importance of the parcels is illustrated. (USAFA, SMS 329)

Stalag Luft 3 -   (10)

Personal Parcels -

1. Prisoners are surprised to note the <u>limiting of personal parcels which are no longer being sent by the British Red Cross, but which are continuing to be sent by the Canadian and American Red Cross.</u>

2. It often happens that parcels announced do not arrive at the camp and others often arrive which have not been advised.

3. Officers are pleased to receive all personal parcels but they would thank the Committee to inform the national Red Cross Societies as to what is adequate and useful in camps. <u>The mixing of soap and foodstuffs should be avoided</u> as the latter are not eatable on arrival when this occurs.

The officers have drawn up three lists of suggested contents for personal parcels which would be of great use in an officers camp

(a) <u>First personal parcel</u> -

    Razor blades   Underwear - Summer
    Tooth brush   Socks - Woollen
    Tooth powder or paste Handkerchiefs
    Towel - Bath   Comb
    Washcloth   Heavy scarf
    Pyjamas   Gloves
    Slippers

(b) <u>Second personal parcel</u> -

    Trousers (green)   Oxfords
    Shirt   "   Complete insignia
    Athletic shorts   Sweater
    Athletic supporter   Flight cap (green)
    Sneakers   Auto pencil and lead
    Cheap watch   Playing cards

(c) <u>Other food parcels</u> -

    Baking powder   Rice
    Cake mixes   Dried apricots
    Spices (cinnamon, nut- Macaroni
    meg etc. no salt or   Bisquick
    pepper)   Tomatoes - dehydrated
    Onion flakes   Cocoa
    Saccharine   Nuts and candy
                          Whole beans

4. The South Africans require tobacco and complain of not having received the tobacco they ordered. They prefer South African to British tobacco.

5. The officers request that national Red Cross societies should insist upon each personal parcel being accompanied by an exact list of contents; thirty per cent of the parcels arriving from Canada contained no lists.

An extract from an International Committee of the Red Cross report, 21 December 1944, on Stalag Luft III. These reports were sent to both the German and Allied governments via the respective Swiss embassies. (*USAFA, SMS 792*)

A visit by Henry Soderberg of the YMCA to the North Compound. (*Left to right*) Major Gustav Simoleit (Camp Second-in-Command), Squadron Leader Bill Jennens (*with his back to the camera*) (POW Adjutant), Group Captain Martin Massey (Senior British Officer), Henry Soderberg, Colonel Friedrich von Lindeiner (Camp Commandant). (*IWM, HU 20998*)

Henry Soderberg also helped POWs with their personal problems. This extract from his British Roster shows some of the requests he dealt with. The bottom entry for Group Captain Alfred Willetts, Senior British Officer of the East Compound from October 1943, is not all it seems, however. He was actually passing coded messages to MI9 back in London, but doing this through the YMCA was against the spirit of the Geneva Convention. (*USAFA, SMS 25*)

```
WILKINSON, Arthuer, 22705, Capt.Dr., Stalag 344
          2.12.43. Wanted a watch. Wife: 423, Fulhem Road, Chelsea, London.
          4.4.44  Gave him watch.

WILLAN, Frank Andrew, Squadr.Ld., 260,  Sta.ag Luft 3
          Mrs. Legation of Denmark at Berlin greets. Parents worried, as they have
          heard nothing. 26.4.44 Feels very well. Has received letters and hopes
          that his letters arrive. - Mr. R.H.Willan, Bridges, Teffont,Salisbury,
          Wilts, Engl.

WILLETTS, A.H., G.Capt., Stalag Luft 3
          26.4.44 Worried about children. Try contact through London. Children are
          staying at "Sant Nichola's school", Fleet Hants, England. Lawyer Lewis-
          Lewis, 10 Ely Place, Holborn.
          June 1944 Received a long cable from London.
          5.12.44 Wanted cable to Mrs. J.Lee Guinness 48, Lowndes Sq, London S.W.
```

Chapter Four

Daily Life

The Germans gave the POWs a degree of autonomy. Each compound had a Senior Allied Officer who was held responsible by the Germans for the conduct of the prisoners in the compound. He also paid close attention to their welfare and well-being. The Germans provided each SAO with an office and a typewriter, and he had weekly meetings with the other SAOs and held discussions with the Commandant and Deputy Commandant when the need arose. The SAOs were also responsible for raising issues with the Red Cross, the Protecting Power and the YMCA. Subordinate to the SAOs were the hut leaders.

Every new prisoner entering the camp was thoroughly searched, especially for items that might be used for escaping. His details were documented on a card and he was given a camp identity disc. He would then be allocated a room in a barrack hut, often in accordance with the advice of the compound adjutant. During his first few days he would also be closely questioned by his peers to ensure that he was not a stool pigeon.

The prisoners' day was bound by the morning and evening *Appel* (roll-call). This was held on the sports field unless the weather was inclement, when it would be held in the barrack huts. Beforehand, each hut leader had to submit a piece of paper to the adjutant, giving the number of his men on parade, plus where the absentees were, e.g. working in the kitchens, sick, etc. The parade formed up under the adjutant in a hollow square grouped by huts and in files of five. The adjutant handed over to the *Lageroffizier* and the counting began. While one German checker counted from the front, another was simultaneously counting from behind. Other Germans would be checking up on the sick and those working elsewhere. If the figures did not tally with the adjutant's, the whole process would be repeated. The figures were also checked with those held by Major Simoleit's department.

Once morning *Appel* was over, it was time for breakfast. The German ration, as has been previously stated, was not sufficient to keep an active male medically fit. It was therefore considerably augmented by Red Cross parcels. Messing was done by rooms, with the inmates taking it in turns to be the duty cook. Each barrack hut did have a cooking stove, but its size was insufficient to cater for the needs of all the rooms. Hence, a strict rota was organised, with each room cook being allowed

30 minutes at the stove. The cooks therefore had to be nimble when it was their turn at the stove and developed an ability to create dishes in the shortest possible time. Cooking utensils were also limited and the POWs had to make their own. The foodstuffs provided by the Germans were bread, potatoes and soup, which was the lunchtime staple, with hardly anything in the way of green vegetables. The prisoners did attempt to cultivate their own, obtaining seeds from the Red Cross, but this was never sufficient to provide vegetables on a regular basis. One scheme involving Red Cross parcels was started as a private enterprise in the East Compound just a few months after the camp had been established. POWs who had items in their parcels which they did not want could exchange them for points. They could then use the points to purchase food which was more to their liking. The scheme was then made a non-profit operation and was adopted in every compound, becoming known as Foodaco, short for Food Account.

Breakfast would typically consist of two slices of bread with some form of spread. Lunch, usually at midday, would be soup and another slice of bread. Supper would be the main meal of the day and might consist of canned meat, potatoes, sometimes vegetables – and the inevitable slice of bread. Coffee or tea would be drunk with all meals. After evening *Appell*, when the prisoners were confined to their huts, they might also have a snack, with coffee or cocoa. But even with the help of the Red Cross parcels, the POWs were often hungry.

With such a large number of men, mostly in their twenties and very active, being cooped up cheek by jowl and surrounded by barbed wire, many could have been driven to insanity. As it was, there were relatively few cases of what was called wire psychosis. The reason for this was that many means of occupying the prisoners' minds and keeping them physically fit were developed. Many spent time planning and putting into practice means of escaping, of which more later. Sport, too, played a major part, with equipment provided by the YMCA and the Red Cross. Soccer, rugby and cricket were popular in the British compounds, as were softball and American football in the American compounds. In addition, volleyball and basketball were also played. Athletics, boxing and fencing were enjoyed, while a number of makeshift golf courses were built, using balls made out of old shoe leather.

The compound theatres were widely supported, putting on a wide range of entertainment, from Shakespeare through musicals to variety shows. The POWs included a number of professional actors, as well as people with behind-stage experience, and the quality of the productions was generally very high. Some of the costumes were made, but many were provided by the YMCA and the Germans, often from opera houses. Sometimes the prisoners had to pay for them. Music, too, played its part. At the simplest level gramophone concerts were very popular, but compounds could also boast everything from symphony orchestras to string quartets, jazz and swing bands. Occasionally films were shown, courtesy of the YMCA. The Centre and South

Compounds also ran their own local 'radio' stations, using the public address loudspeaker system. In addition, some compounds produced their own newspapers. Another outlet was study. Among the inmates were a number of academics and linguists, and those able to teach for professional qualifications, such as accountancy and architectural design. Courses were therefore set up and, through the offices of the Red Cross, the prisoners could sit exams in order to obtain professional qualifications.

Model making was a popular pastime and many prisoners also learnt to draw and paint. One aspect of camp life that might have caused serious problems was alcohol. This was recognised by both the Germans and the prisoners themselves, and alcohol was not sold in any form. However, the making of illicit alcohol or 'hooch' did take place. The main ingredient was dried fruit from Red Cross parcels, which was fermented and distilled to produce a very powerful spirit. Its potency was widely recognised and it only made an appearance on very special occasions such as Christmas and New Year's Eve.

On occasion, small groups of prisoners were allowed outside the wire to take walks in the surrounding area. They had to give their parole not to escape, but still had guards with them.

Under Article 23 of the 1929 Geneva Convention, officer POWs were entitled to have some of their pay transferred to Germany in the form of Reichsmarks, the proviso being that they could not receive more than a German officer of equivalent rank was paid. Other ranks did not have this benefit. The RAF officer inmates were aware that the NCOs had no source of ready income and from very early on they established a Command Fund, to which each officer contributed a third of his transferred pay. Some of this money was used to help the NCOs in Centre Compound. When they moved out, there were also the other ranks who acted as batmen to the officers to take care of. The same applied to the American compounds. The Command Fund was also used to pay for barrack repairs, the cost of theatrical productions and the purchase of furniture from the Germans. In addition, it also enabled the Compound Escape Committees to purchase items from the German canteen. The American compounds employed a similar system.

Dulag Luft at Oberursel, where many Allied aircrew began their captivity as they underwent intelligence questioning. (USAFA, SMS 329)

On arrival at the camp, a new POW had to be photographed. This is Sergeant Frank Newman, who was shot down and injured in August 1944. Unusually for an NCO, he ended up in Belaria. (Jon Wilkinson)

(**Opposite, above**) He was also issued with an identity disc bearing his camp number ... (Jon Wilkinson)

(**Opposite, below**) ... and an identity card. (USAFA, SMS 99)

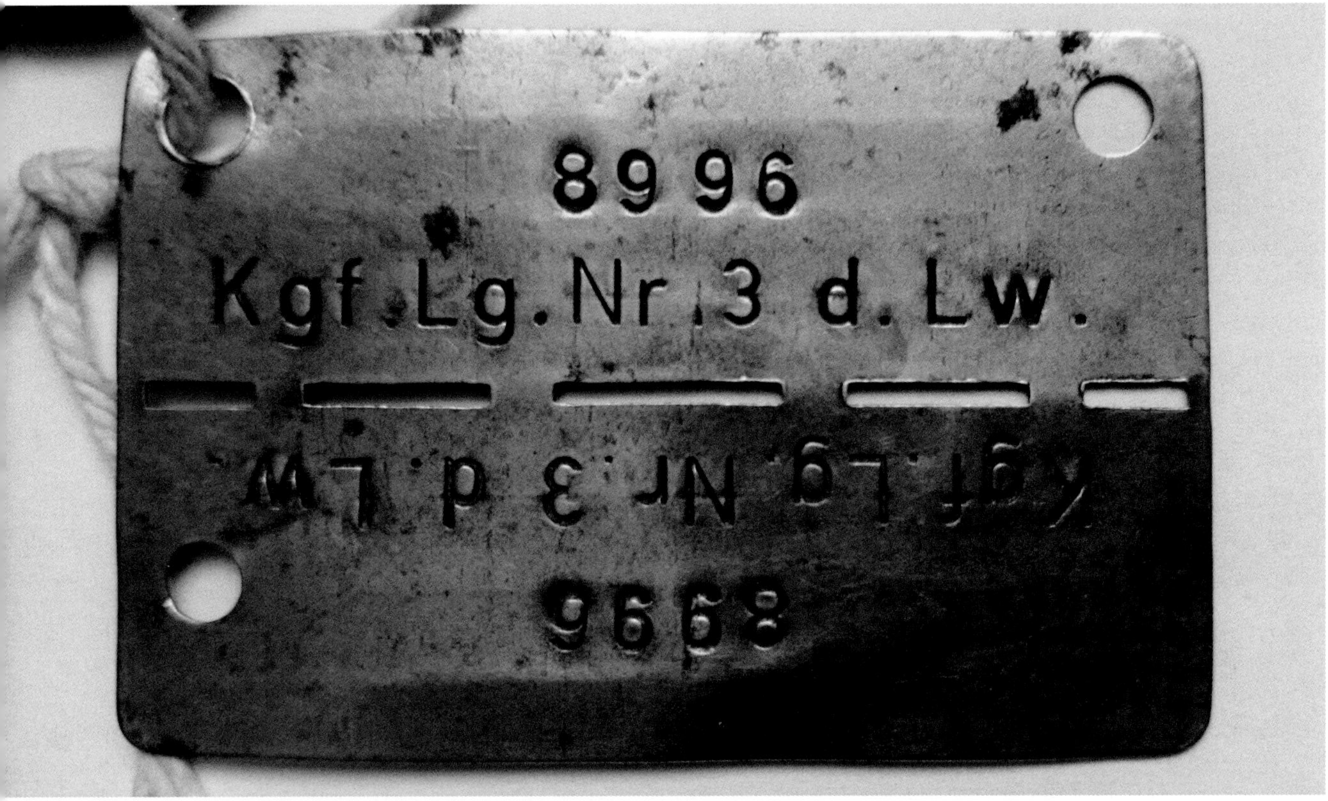
8996
Kgf.Lg.Nr.3 d.Lw.

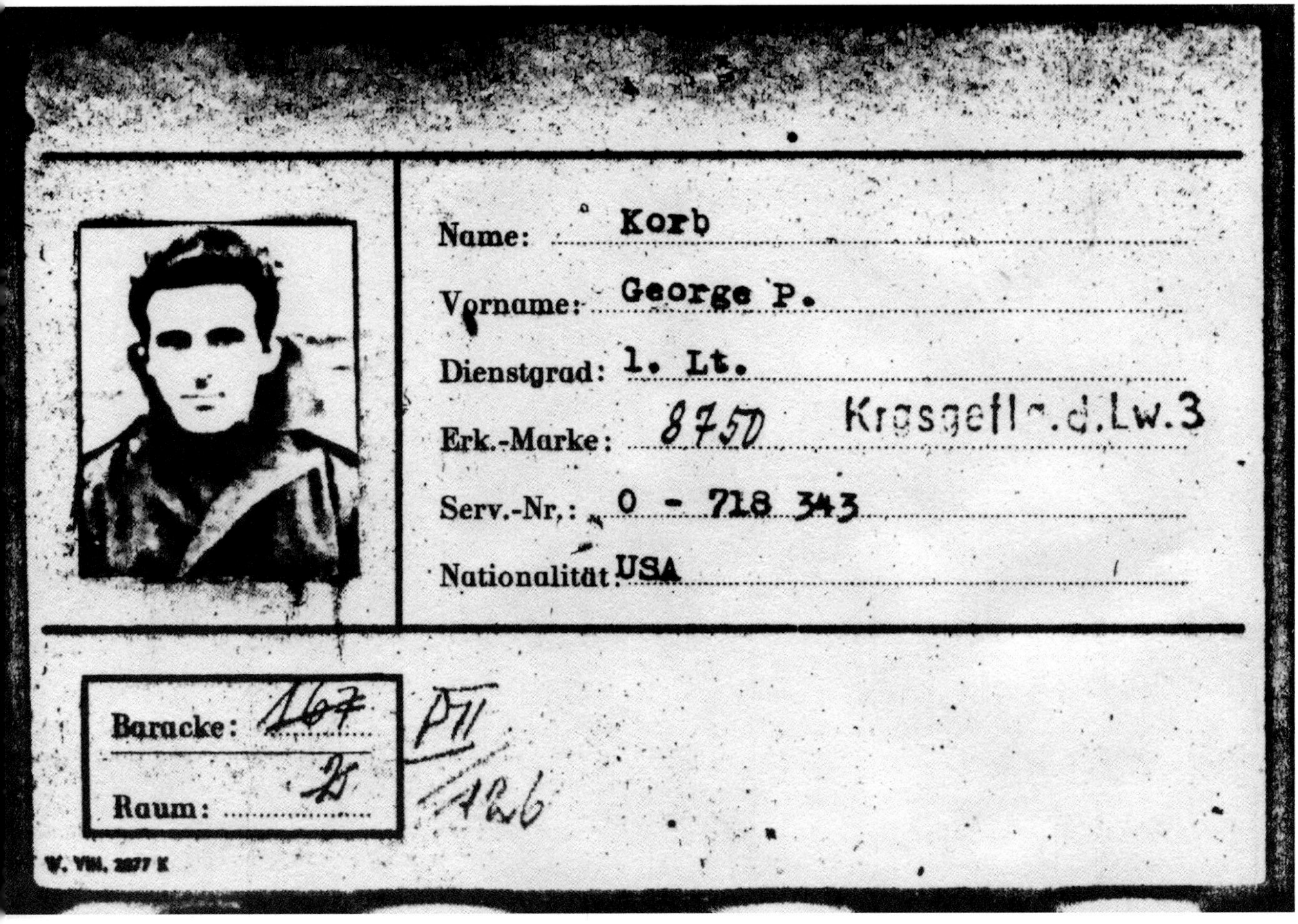

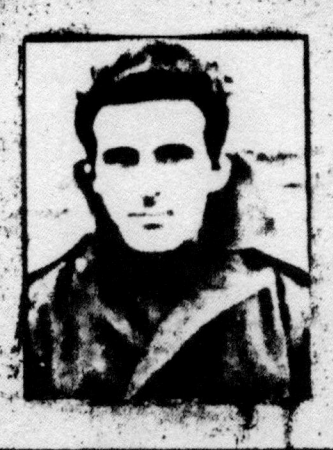

Name: Korb

Vorname: George P.

Dienstgrad: 1. Lt.

Erk.-Marke: 8750 Krgsgefl .d.Lw.3

Serv.-Nr.: 0 - 718 343

Nationalität USA

Baracke: ~~167~~ PII

Raum: 2 126

W. VIII, 2077 K

(**Opposite**) Forming up for morning *Appel* in the South Compound. (**Above**) A German officer taking over the parade. (**Below**) Dispersing after *Appel*. (*USAFA, SMS 329*)

Additional *Appels* were used when it was known that prisoners had escaped and also as a punishment. Here the POWs are being made to show their issue cutlery, mugs and bowls. *(USAFA, SMS 329)*

The morning queue for hot water outside the cookhouse. *(USAFA, SMS 329)*

One cabbage, when available, and 200g of sausage were each man's ration per week. (*USAFA, SMS 329*)

German ration bread. Each POW was allowed 2.425kg of this bread per week. It was dense and very hard to cut. (*USAFA, SMS 329*)

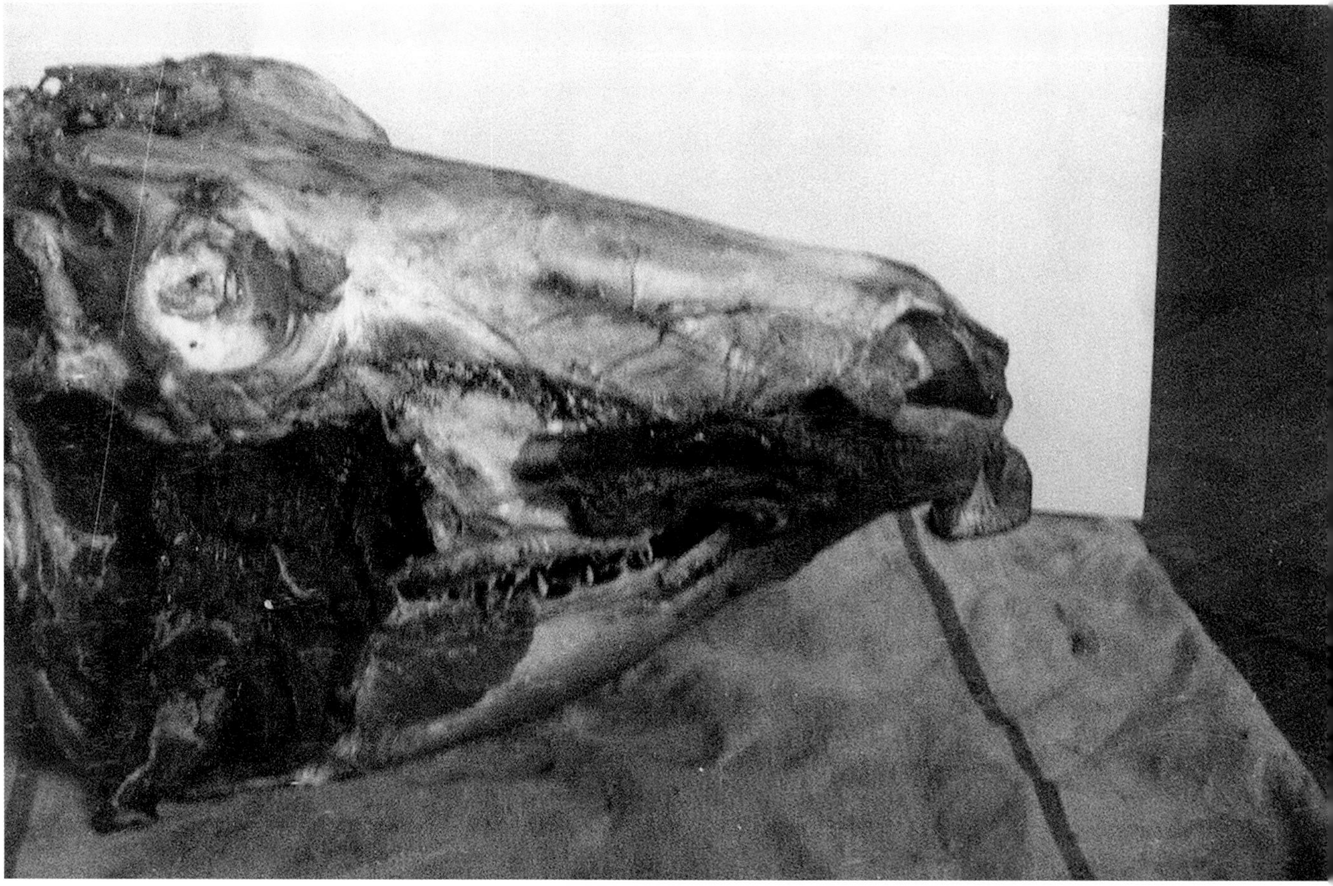

What meat the Germans did provide was often horse, which was boiled as part of the issue soup. (USAFA, SMS 329)

The potatoes were of variable quality. (USAFA, SMS 329)

Occupational therapy – repairing a path in the South Compound ... and the end result; an improvement in the quality of life. *(USAFA, SMS 329)*

Ice hockey in the South Compound. During the winter, ice hockey became as popular with the British as it was with the Americans. All the equipment was supplied by the YMCA, as was the case for most other sports. (*USAFA, SMS 329*)

Watching a sporting event in the North Compound. It was not unusual for officers on the camp staff to attend, as they did theatre productions. (*USAFA, SMS 329*)

Pounding the perimeter to keep both fit and warm. (*USAFA, SMS 329*)

Belles of the South Compound theatre. (*USAFA, SMS 329*)

A country & western show in the South Compound. *(USAFA, SMS 329)*

A performance of *Arsenic and Old Lace*. There was not just talent among the actors, but behind the scenes as well, as this stage set demonstrates. This play, a highly successful black comedy, only opened on Broadway in January 1941. It shows how abreast the prisoners were with contemporary theatre. *(Australian War Memorial)*

Advertising the latest South Compound theatre production. (*USAFA, SMS 329*)

Summer evening concert in the South Compound. (*USAFA, SMS 329*)

The South Compound's 'Luft Bandsters', with instruments courtesy of the YMCA. The band's director had played with Paul Whiteman and his Orchestra, one of the most famous bands of the 1920s and 1930s. (*USAFA, SMS 329*)

In the North Compound the organisers of an arts & crafts exhibition consider items offered up. (*Australian War Memorial*)

A Royal Australian Air Force barrack room. Note the well-stocked bookshelves. Stalag Luft III ended up with extensive libraries, thanks to the Red Cross and national charities. The Germans, however, censored books to ensure that they did not contain material that might aid escapes or encourage sabotage of the German war effort. (*Australian War Memorial*)

This shows how crowded a barrack room could become, but there do not appear to have been many instances of major squabbles ending in violence, brought about by the inevitable tensions of living cheek by jowl. (*USAFA, SMS 329*)

American and British POWs on a parole walk outside the camp, July 1943. As the number of prisoners increased in the camp, these walks became less and less frequent and ceased altogether in March 1944 after the Great Escape. *(USAFA, SMS 329)*

Each compound did have a small canteen, but what it sold was limited, including a rather unpopular German non-alcoholic beer. *(USAFA, SMS 329)*

Prisoner ingenuity – a home-made coffee percolator. (USAFA, SMS 329)

The Germans issued each barrack room with a large jug and bowl. Individual POWs were each given a spoon and fork, cup, mess tin and small bowl. (USAFA, SMS 329)

The RAF-operated food bank in the North Compound. This was run like a canteen, but required paperwork in order to calculate each man's credit after cashing in unwanted Red Cross food items. (*USAFA, SMS 329*)

Another example of POW ingenuity – a home-made printing press. (*USAFA, SMS 329*)

Chopping up wood for the room stoves. Each compound, as it opened, was littered with tree stumps, which the prisoners were left to remove in order to create sports fields. The process did, however, provide fuel and warming exercise in winter. (*USAFA, SMS 329*)

Celebrating US Independence Day with a craps game. Gambling was generally discouraged, especially for money. In this case, the currency was chocolate and cheroots. (*USAFA, SMS 329*)

Some prisoners, like these RAF members, adopted a deliberately scruffy look. Others did their best to remain smart at all times. (*USAFA, SMS 329*)

The burial of an American prisoner. The Germans would also provide a firing party. (*USAFA, SMS 329*)

Another view of a funeral of an American POW. The cemetery was outside the camp, but deaths were not common. (USAFA, SMS 329)

Group Captain Massey, SBO North Compound, dictating orders. (USAFA, SMS 329)

Dutch prisoners celebrate Queen Wilhelmina's birthday. 'Wings' Day is seated in the middle as an honoured guest. (*Vanderstok*)

A typical group of American POWs from the South Compound. (*USAFA, SMS 329*)

A mixed group of RAF and US Army Air Force prisoners in the North Compound. (*USAFA, SMS 329*)

Chapter Five

Prisoner Personalities

Squadron Leader Roger Bushell
A lawyer by profession, Bushell joined the part-time Royal Auxiliary Air Force in 1931. Soon after the outbreak of war in 1939 he was appointed to command 92 Squadron RAF. It was initially equipped with Blenheim fighter-bombers, but converted to Spitfires in March 1940. On 23 May 1940 he was shot down near Boulogne and taken to Dulag Luft at Oberursel for interrogation. There he met up with Wing Commander 'Wings' Day (*see below*), among others, and quickly became involved in escape planning and sending coded intelligence messages back to Britain. At the end of May 1941 there was a break-out through a tunnel at Oberursel. Bushell was one of the escapers, but he did not use the tunnel, choosing instead to hide in a goat shed on the sports field and, after dark, climbing over the single strand of wire guarding it. He reached the Swiss border before being apprehended. All the other escapers were also caught and were sent to Stalag Luft I at Barth, close to the Baltic coast. Bushell was once more involved in escape preparations, especially the digging of tunnels, and in teasing the German guards, a practice known as 'goon baiting'.

In September 1941 Bushell, along with other perceived troublemakers, was transferred to Oflag XC at Lübeck, an army camp in which the conditions were grim. He did not stay long there. The RAF POWs were told that they were to be moved to another camp at Warburg in central Germany. They were taken there by train, but while en route Bushell and a Czech in the RAF escaped. They managed to reach Prague, where Bushell spent the next six months hidden by the Czech Resistance. He was eventually betrayed and arrested by the Gestapo. He was delivered to Stalag Luft III, but was only there for a short while before being taken to Berlin, where he was interrogated over his activities in Prague. After three months the Luftwaffe managed to reclaim him and he was returned to Stalag Luft III.

By now the East Compound had a well organised escape committee. In October 1942, however, 'Wings' Day and other key members were temporarily moved and so Bushell was put in charge of escape activities, becoming known as Big X. As such he planned the famous Great Escape, but was one of the fifty escapees who were subsequently murdered by the Gestapo. He was a larger than life character who made an impression on everyone he came across.

Bob Stanford-Tuck (*left*) and Roger Bushell. Both are clearly wearing Red Cross-issued uniform, since Stanford Tuck has no wings or medal ribands and Bushell is wearing an observer's brevet instead of wings.

Lieutenant Colonel Albert P. Clark

Graduating from the US Military Academy West Point in 1936, Clark joined the Army Air Corps to train as a fighter pilot. With the rapid expansion of the Corps after the fall of France in June 1940, Clark received accelerated promotion. By the spring of 1942, as a 29-year-old lieutenant colonel, he was the Executive Officer of the 31st Fighter Group (equivalent to an RAF Wing). In June 1942 the Group deployed to Britain, the first American fighter unit to do so. On arrival, it was equipped with the Spitfire VB. That July, Clark, together with other key members of the Group, was attached to the RAF Tangmere Wing to gain operational experience. After taking part in ship protection patrols over the English Channel, he carried out his first fighter sweep over northern France on 26 July. After a tussle with four Fockewulf Fw190s, Clark was forced to crash-land close to Cap Gris Nez and became one of the first American aircrew to be captured. After a spell at Oberursel, he was taken to Stalag Luft III and placed in the East Compound. He was initially the subject of some curiosity among the British inmates, but was quickly accepted by them. Clark soon became involved in sending coded messages to MI9 and initiated a successful

Lieutenant Colonel Albert P. Clark, as a prisoner, and his downed Spitfire. (*USAFA, SMS 329*)

campaign to improve hygiene in the compound. He also became involved in escaping. On being moved to the North Compound, when it opened in March 1943, Clark was put in charge of security while the tunnels for the Great Escape were being dug. Unfortunately for him, in September 1943 all the Americans were moved to the newly constructed Centre and South Compounds, with Clark going to the latter. There he took control of escape and intelligence-gathering activities. The latter included coordinating the operation of secret cameras (sent in ordinary parcels by the US Army) for recording all activities in the camp. Clark took part in the long march westwards after the camp was evacuated in January 1945, and ended up in the camp at Moosburg. He remained in the Air Force after the war, rising to the rank of lieutenant general. His last position was Superintendent of the US Air Force Academy and he was instrumental in establishing the Stalag Luft III archive, part of the Academy's Special Collections. Many of the photographs in this book are included by courtesy of General Clark.

Wing Commander Harry 'Wings' Day

Day was originally commissioned into the Royal Marines in 1916. He served afloat and two days before the Armistice had his ship sunk under him but not before he had saved two injured men who were trapped below deck. For this he was awarded the Albert Medal (now the George Cross). In 1924 he joined the Fleet Air Arm, which was soon subsumed by the RAF. He was given a permanent commission as a flight lieutenant in 1930 and gained a reputation as a highly skilled pilot, hence his nickname. Shortly before the outbreak of the Second World War, Day was promoted wing commander and given command of 57 Squadron, which was equipped with Blenheim light bombers. He took his squadron to France as part of the Air Component of the British Expeditionary Force, but was shot down in October 1939 while on a reconnaissance flight. He was one of the first inmates of Dulag Luft and was Senior British Officer there. Day was soon involved in escape activities, principally in digging a tunnel which began next to his room. In late May 1941 he and and seventeen others used this tunnel to escape. He was captured

A post-war photograph of 'Wings' Day.

two days later and together with the other escapers, including Roger Bushell, was sent to Stalag Luft I. There he created an escape organisation which would be used in many other POW camps. In March 1942 the camp was closed and the inmates transferred to Stalag Luft III. Day made two escape attempts from there before being sent to Oflag XXIB in Schubin. After a further abortive escape, he was returned to Stalag Luft III, where he became deeply involved with the Great Escape, managing to reach the port of Stettin (today Szczecin) before he was betrayed by a French POW and fell into the hands of the Gestapo. After interrogation, he was sent, together with three other escapers, to Sachsenhausen concentration camp. This did not deter him, and he and others dug another tunnel, through which they escaped. Again he was caught and this time he was incarcerated in Sachsenhausen's death cells. In February 1945 he was moved to Dachau and then, in April, to the Tyrol, the Germans having an idea that he and other prominent prisoners could be used as bargaining counters when negotiating with the Allies. Even then he again escaped, using a stolen car to reach the Allied lines in northern Italy to inform them of the hostage situation. For his conduct as a POW Day was awarded the DSO and made an OBE. The Americans also honoured him with the Legion of Merit. He remained in the RAF until 1950.

Sergeant James 'Dixie' Deans

A Whitley pilot in 77 Squadron, Deans was shot down over Holland in September 1940. He was initially sent to Stalag Luft I, where his powers of leadership were quickly recognised and he was elected Camp Leader by his fellow NCOs. He was with the first group to arrive at Stalag Luft III in April 1942. Placed in the Centre Compound, which housed the non-commissioned POWs, Deans was once again elected as Compound Leader, or, as the Germans termed him, 'the man of confidence'. Unlike the SAOs of the officer compounds, Deans had no disciplinary powers and, in fact, was junior in rank to a number of his fellow inmates. Yet through the sheer force of his personality he got the compound running on organised lines. He also quickly gained the respect of the Germans, including the camp commandant. He organised the writing of coded letters back to the UK through the auspices of MI9. A secret radio had been brought into the camp from Stalag Luft I and Deans used bribery to get a German guard to supply parts for it. This enabled the POWs to obtain news from the BBC. When the Centre Compound was occupied by American POWs in June 1943, Deans and many others were moved to Stalag Luft VI at Heydekrug, Lithuania. There Deans operated as before, as he did later at Stalag Luft IV, to which he was sent after Stalag Luft VI was evacuated in July 1944 in the face of Russian advances. Day's greatest challenge came in early 1945 during the so-called Long March westwards. He found himself with a column of 2,000 POWs en route to a camp at Fallingbostel. Through sheer force of personality, Deans ensured that his men obtained food and shelter, as well as transport for the sick, while on the march. From

Dixie Deans at Stalag Luft I (*back row, second right*).

Fallingbostel they were marched north towards Lübeck, but such was Deans' hold over the Germans that they agreed to him going on ahead to inform the advancing British troops of the presence of the column. Deans ended by taking the surrender of the German guard commander. He was made an MBE for his work, although many felt that he should have received greater recognition. He later became the first President of the RAF Ex-POWs Association, but suffered for many years from multiple sclerosis.

Colonel Charles G. 'Rojo' Goodrich

Goodrich graduated from West Point in 1928 and joined the Army Air Corps. During the next twelve years he was stationed at various bases in America and Panama. Then in January 1941 he was given command of the newly activated 12th (Light) Bomber Group, which was based in Washington State. In March 1942 the Group moved to Louisiana to train on the new B-25 Mitchell bomber and in late July of the same year it was deployed to Egypt as part of the Ninth Army Air Force, flying missions in support

of the British forces. In mid-September Goodrich was shot down over Libya and broke his back while baling out. After stays in four Axis hospitals en route, he ended up in Stalag Luft III in February 1943. He was initially the SAO in the North Compound and undertook the same role when the South Compound was opened in September that year. After the Long March, Goodrich was incarcerated in Stalag VIIA at Moosburg from where he was liberated. Repatriated to the USA in July 1945, he remained in the Air Force for a further ten years.

Colonel 'Rojo' Goodrich, Senior American Officer in the North and then South Compounds. (USAFA)

Group Captain Martin Massey

Commissioned into the infantry in 1916, Massey transferred to the Royal Flying Corps and joined 16 Squadron in France that July as a pilot flying BE2es. Promoted flight commander, he was shot down in February 1917, suffering burns and losing half a leg. He was awarded the MC and spent the rest of the war in Britain, but was granted a permanent commission in the RAF in 1919, in spite of being an amputee. He rose steadily and in 1934 took command of 6 Squadron. In 1936 he deployed with his squadron to the Middle East and was involved in containing the Arab revolt in Palestine. He was again wounded, but earned the DSO. Promoted group captain in 1940, he became station commander of first RAF Abingdon and then RAF Oakington. He still flew on the occasional operation and on the night of 1/2 June 1942 he was shot down over the Dutch coast when part of a Stirling bomber crew. He ended up in Stalag Luft III, where he became SBO of the East Compound until April 1943, when he assumed the same position in the North Compound. As such, he was responsible for authorising the Great Escape and was portrayed in the film of the same name as Group Captain Ramsey. His wounds continued to give him trouble and he spent several periods in hospital. Eventually, in May 1944, he was repatriated and was able to alert the authorities in Britain to the murders that had resulted from the Great Escape. He continued to serve in the RAF after the war, retiring as an air commodore.

Colonel Delmar T. Spivey

A 1928 graduate of West Point, he initially served as an infantryman before transferring to the Army Air Corps in 1930. During the next decade he was both pilot and engineer. Then followed two postings to the Air Corps Proving Ground before Spivey took on another speciality: air gunnery. In May 1942 he took command of the Flexible Gunnery School. Drawing on RAF experience and existing manuals, he began to develop new tactics. On hearing that graduates of his school were displaying an inability to hit targets when on operations, he visited the Eighth Army Air Force in Britain to find out why. On 12 August 1943 he went on his first operational mission in a B-17 in order to establish what was going wrong. The target was the Ruhr, which was reached, but the plane was then struck by flak. It turned for home, but was eventually forced to crashland close to the German–Dutch border. After being interrogated at Dulag Luft, Spivey arrived at Stalag Luft III twelve days after he was shot down. After two weeks under the wing of Colonel Goodrich in the North Compound, Spivey took over as SAO in the Centre Compound. It had been recently vacated by the NCOs and the infrastructure was in a poor state of repair. Spivey's drive ensured that the compound became more habitable, but it never reached the standard of the other compounds because the original construction had been so poor. He also organised a comprehensive daily log, covering all aspects of camp life, to be written so that future generations of POWs would not have to 'reinvent the wheel'. During the Long March he accompanied General Vanaman (*see below*) to Berlin and went with him to Switzerland. The end of the war in Europe found him at Eisenhower's headquarters. He rose to the rank of major general and retired in 1956.

Colonel Delmar T. Spivey, Senior American Officer in the Centre Compound. (*USAF*)

Wing Commander Bob Stanford Tuck

Stanford Tuck joined the RAF in 1935. At the outbreak of war he was with 65 Squadron flying Spitfires but it was not until early May 1940, when he transferred to 92 Squadron, commanded by Roger Bushell, that he first saw action. He distinguished himself in the skies over Dunkirk, earning the first of his DFCs. He increased his tally during the first half of the Battle of Britain, although he was shot down once and on another occasion was forced to crash-land after his engine had been hit. In September 1940 he was given command of a Hurricane squadron, No. 257. He led this for the next ten months, winning two more DFCs and the DSO. He was then promoted wing commander and took charge of the Duxford Wing, flying missions over northern France to draw up the Luftwaffe. In the autumn of 1941 Stanford Tuck took a break from combat flying, visiting the USA to brief the US Army Air Force on fighter tactics. In December 1941 he took command of the Biggin Hill Wing, but was shot down by flak over northern France at the end of the following January. By that time he had amassed 29 confirmed victories, making him one of the RAF's top aces. Sent to Stalag Luft III, he quickly became involved in escape activities. Roger Bushell put him in charge of the supply of materials needed for digging tunnels. He also took part in a number of escape attempts. He had booked his place for the Great Escape when, in January 1944, he and some other POWs were suddenly transferred to Belaria, Stalag Luft III's newly built satellite camp. He took charge of the escape committee there and ran it until the camp was evacuated in January 1945. During the subsequent march westwards, Stanford Tuck and a Polish RAF officer escaped by hiding under straw after an overnight halt. They fell into Russian hands and Stanford Tuck eventually reached Odessa, from where he was repatriated by sea. He remained in the RAF until 1949, when he retired to run a mushroom farm, but not before the Americans awarded him their DFC.

Brigadier General Arthur W. Vanaman

Vanaman was the highest-ranking Allied officer in Stalag Luft III. He enlisted in the Aviation Section of the US Signal Corps in 1917 and from then on specialised as an engineer. In 1937 he became the Assistant Air Attaché in Berlin, serving in this post for four years. Then, after a number of appointments in the USA, in May 1944 Vanaman was made Assistant Chief of Staff (Intelligence) of the Eighth US Army Air Force in Britain. He believed that his intelligence officers should have experienced flying operations and he resolved to set an example. Unfortunately, on 27 June 1944 the B-17 in which he was flying on a mission against V-weapon storage sites in the Pas de Calais had an engine hit by flak. The plane caught fire and the pilot ordered the crew to bale out. Half of them did so, including Vanaman, but the flames then went out and the pilot was able to fly the plane back to base. Vanaman ended up in Stalag Luft III's Centre Compound. Initially, there was some suspicion that he might be a plant, but Vanaman quickly gained the respect of his fellow POWs. The Germans were aware of his time in Berlin and of his contacts and gave him parole to visit the other two US compounds in the camp. He did, however, have to be permanently on his guard since he was privy to Ultra, the Allied ability to read the German Enigma codes. When the Long March began in January 1945 Vanaman led the Centre Compound column. During the journey to Moosburg, he, Spivey and two others were taken to Berlin on the orders of SS General Gottlieb Berger. Vanaman wanted to travel to Switzerland in order to meet the Red Cross and ensure the supply of Red Cross parcels to American POWs. Berger initially agreed to this, but changed his mind as he wanted Vanaman to attend a medical conference on the treatment of POWs in order to give it respectability. He did, however, arrange for Red Cross parcels to be brought into Germany in specially marked trucks. Berger's ulterior motive was to negotiate a separate peace with the Western Allies so that all Germany's armed forces could be used against Russia. He therefore sent Vanaman and Spivey to Switzerland, but by the time they arrived there on 23 April the Allies had no interest in any separate peace deals. Vanaman was, however, flown to Washington, DC to give a report. He remained in the Air Force after the war, holding a number of technical command appointments, before retiring as a major general in the mid-1950s.

Brigadier General Arthur W. Vanaman, the senior Allied POW in Stalag Luft III, taken after the war. (USAF)

Group Captain Alfred Willetts

Commissioned into the RAF in 1925, in 1941 Willetts became the deputy air adviser to the Chief of Combined Operations and carried out the air planning for the highly successful Vaagso commando raid, which was carried out in December 1941. He himself led the bombers and was awarded the DSO. In July 1943 he was appointed station commander of RAF Oakington, following in Martin Massey's footsteps. Like him, Willetts took part in occasional operations and was shot down over Berlin on the night of 23/24 August 1943, while flying in a 7 Squadron Lancaster Pathfinder. Sent to Stalag Luft III, he became SBO of the East Compound in October 1943, remaining in post until the evacuation of the camp in January 1945. During the march westwards Willetts accompanied the East and South Compound contingents and ended up by taking the surrender of the camp at Moosburg. He retired from the RAF shortly after the end of the war, and was awarded the US Bronze Star for his services as a POW.

Chapter Six

The Intelligence War

Stalag Luft III was the scene of a constant battle for intelligence. On the German side, attempts to gain intelligence on the Allies had been carried out through the interrogations of air crew at Dulag Luft. What concerned them at Sagan was thwarting the numerous attempts by the prisoners to escape. It was to this end that the Ferrets were employed, as described in the next section.

From the POW point of view there were three types of intelligence. First was that pertaining to escape, and covering a number of subjects ranging from details on travel and identity documents, through the clothing worn by Germans and foreign workers and what travelling conditions were like, to security details in Stalag Luft III itself. To coordinate the gathering of this information the escape committee in each compound had a head of escape intelligence. The sources were varied. Each new arrival was questioned on what he might have noticed during his journey to the camp. Escapers who had been brought back to the camp, once they had completed their 10–14 days in the cells, were subjected to very close questioning over how they had been caught. Had it been because some of their travel documents were out of date? Had they inadvertently entered a restricted area? Was a safe house no longer safe in that they had been betrayed? Had they boarded the wrong part of a train? If they had reached an international frontier it was important to have details of security on the border, especially where holes in it were. The port of Stettin was of especial interest, since neutral Swedish ships were to be found there and could take escapers to Sweden, provided that they were able to make contact with friendly crew members. Prisoners who were sent to hospital outside the camp or who were involved in the collection of Red Cross parcels and visits to the YMCA store could also provide useful information on local conditions.

Much information was also obtained from the camp guards. The prisoners realised that some were open to being bribed, especially with items such as chocolate and coffee from Red Cross parcels, commodities which were becoming increasingly rare in Germany. Once they had accepted bribes, the guards were compromised and were trapped into co-operating because of the risk of being exposed. The 'contacts', as the prisoners termed them, could give much local information on the Sagan area, as well as items like railway timetables and current travel documents. One major asset was a mole inside the *Kommandantur*. He was a clerk with strong anti-Nazi beliefs and provided much useful information on such topics as impending changes to the guard routine, workers coming into the compounds, and other matters.

The second type of intelligence was military. It had been recognised in the second half of the First World War that POWs could be a very useful source of intelligence on the enemy. Accordingly, in December 1939 the British War Office established a new intelligence branch, MI9. Its purpose was to assist POWs in their efforts to escape, to gather and disseminate information from the POWs and to keep up their morale. In terms of obtaining intelligence through the prisoners, MI9 devised a code which they could use in their letters home. In order to set up the system, lectures were given to small groups of aircrew and those who showed themselves adept at using the code were then registered, with each man given an identity number. Roger Bushell was an early recruit and he was certainly collating information with 'Wings' Day when in Dulag Luft in the summer of 1940. It was only then, however, that he seems to have been introduced to one of MI9's codes, by a shot-down Wellington pilot. In this way knowledge spread and the numbers using the codes increased. The Americans established a similar branch to MI9 called MIS-X. They initially used the British codes, but then developed their own. These, however, were found to be less easy to use and so they reverted to the British system.

As for the information which was of interest to Allied military intelligence, the detailed circumstances in which a newly arrived POW was shot down were important, especially if the Luftwaffe appeared to be using new tactics or weapons. They were also quizzed about anything they might have noted en route to Stalag Luft III, including bomb damage, the location of factories and airfields, and German morale. What the Germans already knew when they came to interrogate shot-down air crew was also of importance in that it might help to establish the sources of their information. Information from recaptured escapers was also very useful, especially if they had been briefed on what to look for prior to their escape. The other major source was the 'contacts' among the camp staff. Troop movements were one topic, given that Sagan had so many railway lines running into it. Bomb damage was another, especially as reported by the contact's family and friends, as well as when he went on leave. Shortages of food, raw materials and fuel, as well as their effect on morale, were also noteworthy.

The information gathered from these sources needed to be collated by the compound's code intelligence officer. He in turn consulted with the compound senior officer, who decided what needed to be transmitted. The resultant messages were then passed to the compound's coding officers, who encoded them. Finally, they were incorporated in letters home written by the code letter writers, the recipients having been briefed by MI9. In this way London and Washington received much valuable information. One particular example concerned the German V-weapons experimental centre at Peenemünde on the Baltic coast.

The third type of intelligence that concerned the POWs was gaining a true picture of the course of the war as a whole. The Germans did supply daily papers, but of course these only gave the Nazi viewpoint and much of the content was thinly disguised propaganda. On the other hand, it was possible, by reading between the lines, to get an idea of conditions within Germany itself, which could be useful as escape intelligence. There was thus a thirst for the truth of what was happening. New arrivals would be closely questioned on what conditions were like at home and what was happening in the war as a whole, but often their information was sketchy. What was needed was a reliable news service and the BBC was the obvious answer, but to listen to it required radio receivers – which of course were forbidden by the Germans. It was the NCOs of the Centre Compound who first had a radio. They had acquired it at Barth and smuggled it into Stalag Luft III when they moved there in the spring of 1942. Indeed, for the next year the officers in the East Compound were totally reliant on this radio for news, important items being passed through the wire using arm semaphore. An East Compound officer who read semaphore then went round all the huts to pass on the information.

The East Compound managed to acquire its own radio in April 1943. To disseminate the news, it was initially taken down in shorthand. This was converted to longhand and then read out to the various huts, after which the papers were destroyed. At first, the North Compound relied on the East Compound for news, but through contacts among the German staff managed to obtain the parts of a so-called German 'People's Set'. This was in operation from July 1943. Other contacts produced a large French set, which was broken down into two smaller sets, one of which was given to the Americans when they occupied the South Compound. The compound also acquired a number of other radios from various sources, including one concealed in a cribbage board and sent by MIS-X. The officers in the Centre Compound procured their first radio by stealing it from their *Vorlager*. By the spring of 1944 both MI9 and MIS-X were communicating with the prisoners via the radios, using specially developed codes. This enabled answers to queries raised by the POWs in their coded letters to be more speedily provided.

The Germans were aware of the secret radios, but very seldom discovered them. Indeed, the prisoners used very ingenious methods to hide them and their location was strictly on a 'need to know' basis. What is certain is that they did much to maintain morale, especially after the war began to turn in favour of the Allies in the autumn of 1942.

Chatting up the Germans could result in them letting slip information, which could be useful as general intelligence or might be relevant to escaping. *(USAFA, SMS 329)*

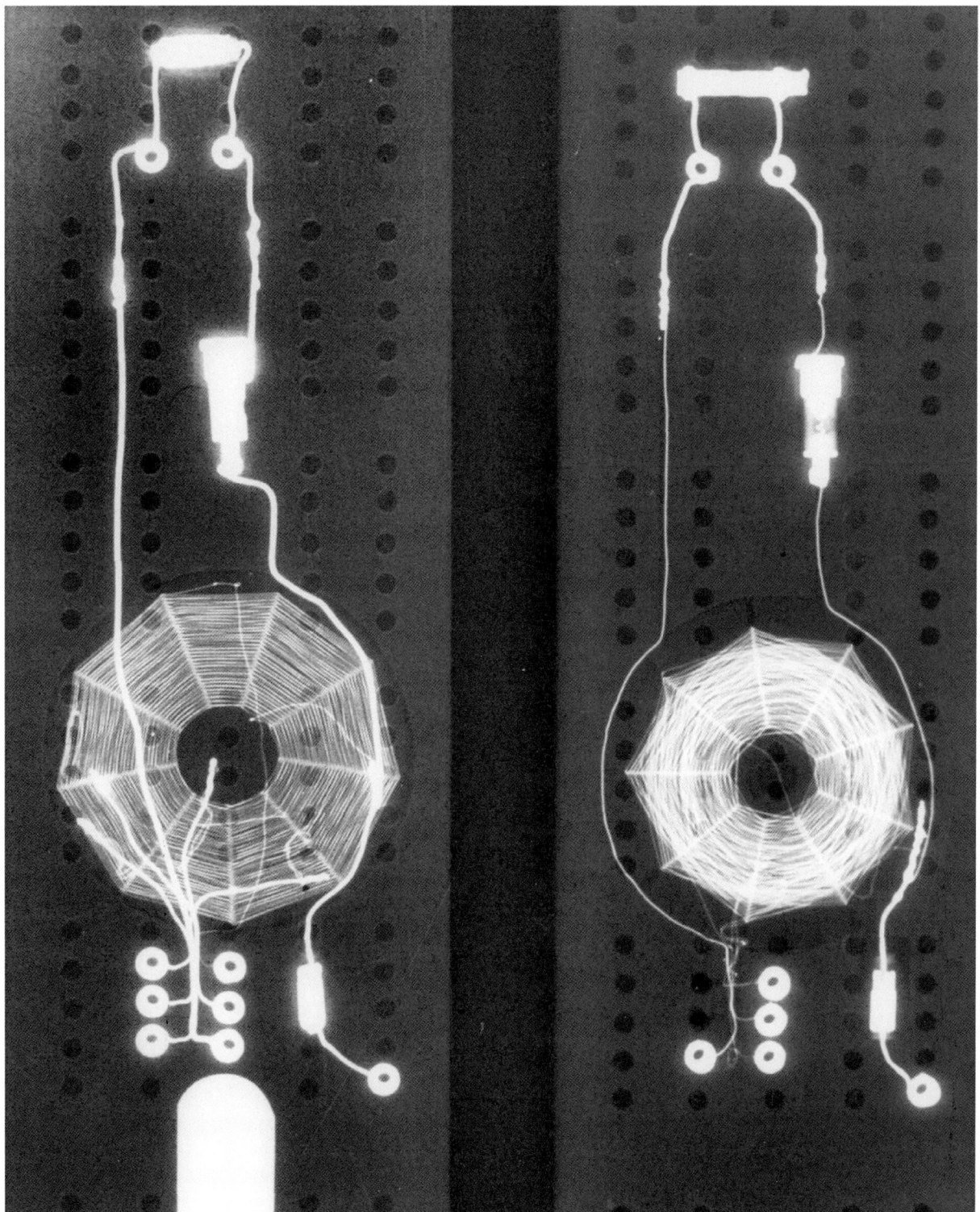
A radio receiver hidden in a cribbage board and sent to Stalag Luft III by MIS-X. (*USAF*)

Tuning in to the BBC News on a clandestine radio set. (*USAFA, SMS 329*)

An American POW cultivating a contact from among the German guards. Besides providing materials in support of escaping, they could also give useful intelligence for passing back to London and Washington, DC. (*USAFA, SMS 329*)

Greeting new arrivals at the camp. While fresh faces were welcome, news of how the war was really going and the fact that they might possess useful intelligence were perhaps more important. *(USAFA, SMS 329)*

Using Morse Code to communicate with a neighbouring compound. Semaphore was also used. *(USAFA, SMS 329)*

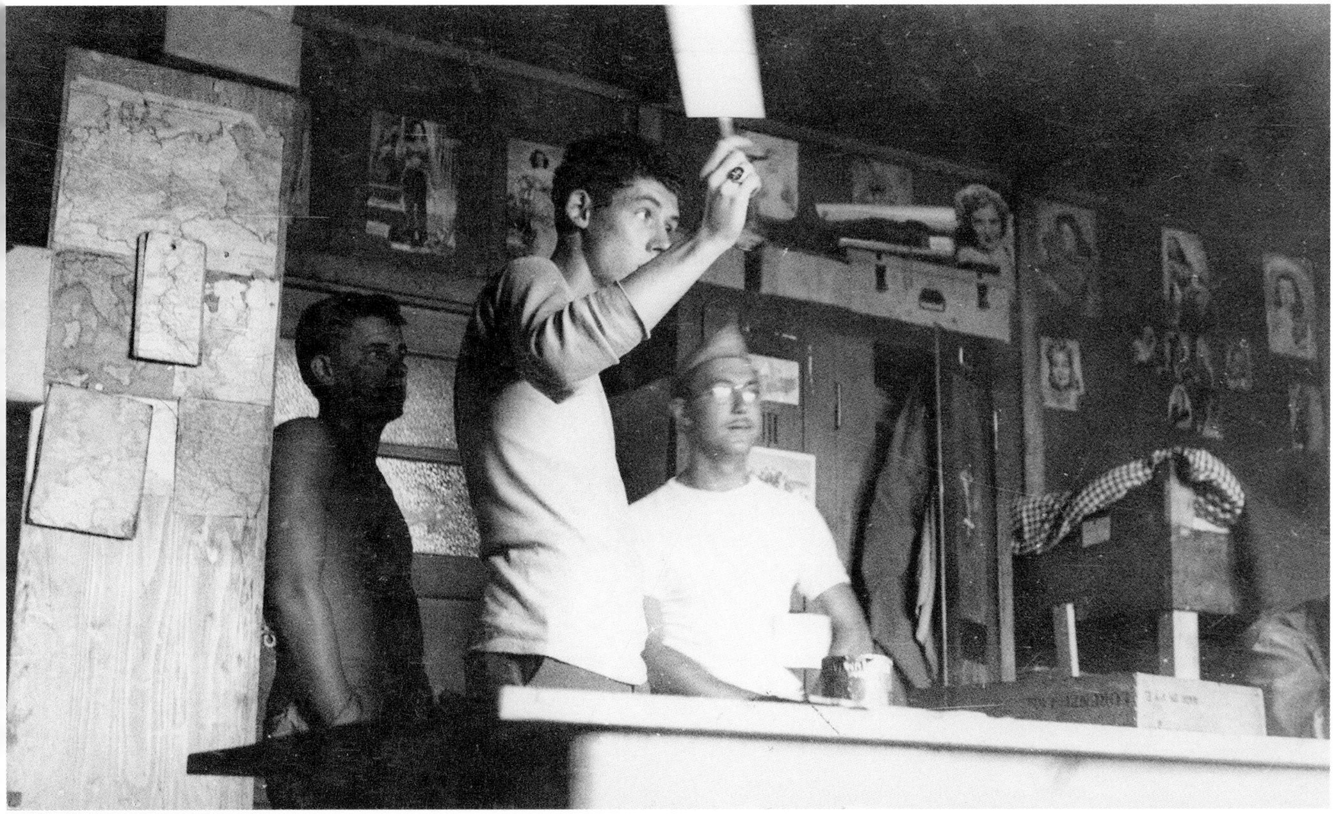

Studying German war communiques and accompanying maps. By reading between the lines it was possible to glean useful intelligence. *(USAFA, SMS 329)*

Chapter Seven

Escaping

Many of the original officer inhabitants of Stalag Luft III arrived in the camp in the spring of 1942 bent on escape. Indeed, as has been described, some had already been involved in escapes from their previous camps, notably Dulag Luft and Stalag Luft I. There was no order *per se* which instructed captured British officers to make every effort to escape, but MI9 certainly did its best to foster this frame of mind. While not every prisoner chose to be involved in escaping, a sizeable proportion were. In part, it was a burning desire to get home and rejoin the war, especially so that their expensive aircrew training could continue to be put to use. At a more mundane level, being involved in escaping helped to fill the hours and take their minds off their predicament.

What the likes of Wing Commander 'Wings' Day had learned was that establishing a proper escape organisation was essential. To allow individuals or small groups to operate on their own in an uncoordinated way inevitably meant failure and a waste of valuable resources. Instead, there should be an escape committee which would consider all escape plans and then put its resources behind those which it believed had the best chance of success. Thus, such an organisation, known as the X Committee, was established in the East Compound from the outset. The NCOs of the Centre Compound also had an escape committee, but this laboured under two disadvantages, even after its leader secretly exchanged with an officer POW for two weeks so that he could be thoroughly briefed on running an X Committee. The first problem was that there was no formal framework of discipline in the NCOs compound, while in the East Compound the SBO was able to delegate powers of discipline to the X Committee. Secondly, only a minority of the NCOs were interested in escaping. This is not to say that no escape attempts were made. They were, but mainly by the warrant officers rather than the NCOs *per se* and none was successful.

As for the escapes themselves, there were three basic types: over the wire, through the wire and under the wire. The first named was the least popular and was really only used in the early days. Some such attempts took advantage of loopholes in the German security system, while others relied on the use of diversions to distract the guards. An increase in the number of guard towers and more frequent German patrols around the outside of the camp perimeter served to make this method of escape ever less attractive.

The second type of escape could mean literally cutting one's way through the wire or getting out via the main gate of the compound. Cutting through the wire needed the same conditions as climbing over it and had the same drawbacks. Trucks and horse-drawn carts visited the compounds frequently, bringing in supplies or workmen and their tools. There were thus opportunities for POWs to smuggle themselves aboard. Often, these were spur of the moment efforts. The other option was to disguise oneself as a German guard or a workman and literally walk through the main gate. This, however, did require a fluent knowledge of German and an understanding of the German character in order to be able to conduct oneself without suspicion.

The most popular method of escape was undoubtedly going under the wire, which meant constructing tunnels. Indeed, during the time that Stalag Luft III was operating as a camp over a hundred were dug. Whereas the other methods of escape tended to be restricted to individual efforts, tunnels presented the prospect of mass escapes, as happened in March 1944. They also involved many more people and for a much longer length of time. There were, too, technical problems to overcome, which challenged the POWs' ingenuity and hence kept their minds occupied.

The escape organisation in each compound became increasingly elaborate and it is worth detailing that which oversaw the Great Escape. At the heart was Big X, Squadron Leader Roger Bushell. He worked closely with the Senior British Officer, Group Captain Martin Massey, who gave all newcomers a talk to make them aware of the escape organisation. He and Bushell also held a weekly meeting with the individual hut escape representatives to discuss current activities. Big X also had a planning committee, which was made up of experts in each type of escape. An individual with an idea for an escape would initially explain it to his hut representative. If the latter thought that there was merit in the scheme, the proposer would be interviewed by the relevant member of the planning committee. He in turn, if he supported the idea, would refer it to Bushell for final approval.

The escape organisation also had a range of experts who sat on its main committee. There was a carpentry expert, whose team created anything from hiding places for escape equipment, through trolleys and rails for tunnels, to dummy rifles for those who intended to masquerade as German guards. Escape food was another aspect. This usually took the form of concentrated nutrition bars made up from the contents of Red Cross parcels. Security was of prime importance to ensure that the Germans did not get wind of escape preparations. Head of Security in the North Compound until the Americans were moved to their own compound was Colonel Albert P. Clark, one of the first American pilots to arrive in Stalag Luft III. During the same period another American also sat on the Escape Committee to represent the interests of his fellow countrymen. Running hand-in-hand with Security, and indeed part of it, was the Duty Pilot scheme. This took its name from the pre-war system on RAF airfields where a duty pilot logged the arrival and departure of aircraft. In this case it was the Germans who were being monitored, especially the Ferrets. The Duty Pilot would alert watchers, known as 'stooges', who would track the movements of the Germans and warn any groups of POWs engaged in escape activities if they got too close. This was a vital job and hence the head Duty Pilot was on the Escape Committee.

Intelligence, too, was an important aspect and the officer in charge of collating it sat on the Committee, as did the officer in charge of the linguists who went through the German newspapers. The officer who ran the Contact organisation was also included. The Germans who had been entrapped by this produced not only intelligence but also items such as cameras, which were used mainly to take identity photographs for the necessary documents that each prisoner would need when on the run. The documents themselves were produced by a highly skilled team of forgers. Such was their dedication that it would sometimes take one man weeks to reproduce a particular document. The forgers also made their own rubber stamps out of shoe heels. Clothing was also represented. Most escapers, but not all, wanted a disguise, either as a German guard (to get them out of the camp) or civilian clothes for their travels across Germany. The favourite disguise was that of a foreign worker, especially since this would help to explain an inability to speak German well. The POW tailors became adept at converting uniform into civilian garments, especially greatcoats. Some clothing items were obtained via the Contacts, particularly badges, insignia, buttons and dyes. The POWs did receive some civilian clothing from home in their two-monthly parcels, but this was usually confiscated by the Germans. The prisoners did, however, manage to steal some back.

An officer in charge of supplies also sat on the Escape Committee. Apart from procuring tools for carpentry and other necessary tasks, he also needed to obtain much wood, especially for shoring up the tunnels. Much of this came in the form of bed-boards from the prisoners' bunks. He also had a team reproducing maps produced by Contacts and MI9. The making of compasses was also carried out, using melted gramophone records for the cases and magnetised steel needles or strips of razor blade. The North Compound alone made some 500 by March 1944. There were, too, engineering problems to be overcome, notably how to ventilate the tunnels and how to establish an effective system for evacuating spoil, which was solved by trolleys on wooden rails.

The Germans, of course, did not remain passive in the face of all this activity. The Ferrets especially were constantly on the prowl, using probes to detect tunnelling, as well as carrying out searches of the huts. In order to better detect tunnelling, microphones were sunk to a depth of 9ft inside the perimeter fence in order to pick up digging noises. Likewise, a 7ft-deep trench was dug in the East Compound, also inside the perimeter fence, with water overflow from the wash-houses allowed into it. All this meant that the tunnels had to be dug deep. To make it more difficult for escapers to get out through the compound gates, a system of special passes and booking in and out was set up, with the Germans holding photographs and descriptions of all known escapers in their guard houses. This was in addition to the details held on each POW by the Abwehr. Colonel von Lindeiner also established a museum in the camp, which covered all aspects of escape, and staff from other camps came to see it in order to learn lessons.

In spite of the Germans' best efforts to prevent escapes taking place, a good number of POWs did manage to get outside the wire. Some were picked up close to the camp and others at Sagan railway station. Several managed to get further afield. They were usually caught out either by being in a restricted zone, or through irregularities in their papers or their lack of linguistic skills. Only six escapers managed to make it back to Britain in what was known as a 'home run'. The remainder, at least up until the Great Escape of March 1944, were usually sent back fairly promptly to Stalag Luft III. There they would be given the standard punishment of fourteen days in the cells (known as the Cooler) or, for persistent escapers, twenty or twenty-one days. They served their time in solitary confinement.

The first question a would-be escaper had to ask himself was 'shall I go over, through, or under the wire?' The woods surrounding the camp did provide initial cover. (USAFA, SMS 329)

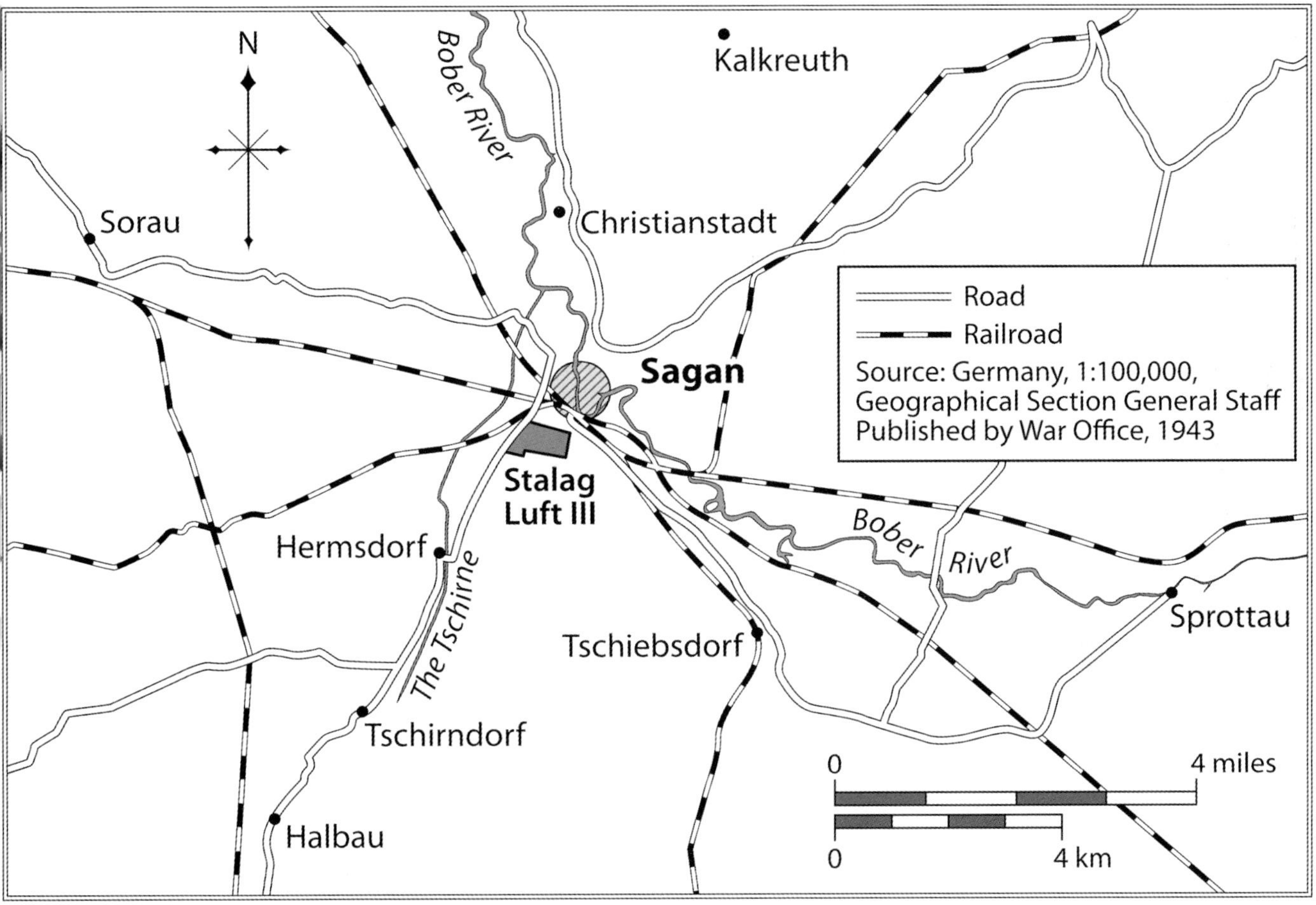

Sagan railway station could not have been more conveniently placed as it was an important junction.

Zagan railway station booking hall today. Apart from the notices being in Polish, rather than in German, it has changed little since the Second World War.

The camp forgers became masters of their trade. A fine example of their work is this Travel Permit for Bram Vanderstok to travel to Alkmaar in his native Holland. It certainly passed muster and helped him to make a successful 'home run'. *(Vanderstok)*

The port of Stettin was a favourite objective of escapers in the hopes of getting aboard a Scandinavian vessel and reaching neutral Sweden.

A foiled through-the-wire escape attempt. Two RAF officers disguised themselves as German guards, with adapted greatcoats and wooden rifles. The giveaway was that their greatcoats were too short, as can be seen when they were put alongside the genuine article. *(USAFA, SMS 329)*

One vehicle which the prisoners did not try to smuggle themselves aboard was the so-called 'Honey Wagon', which took away the latrine waste. *(USAFA, SMS 329)*

Ferrets who have been digging for a tunnel. *(USAF)*

One way of disposing of freshly discovered tunnels was to collapse them using a fire hose, as this Ferret has been doing. (*USAF*)

Two suspicious-looking Ferrets. (*USAFA, SMS 329*)

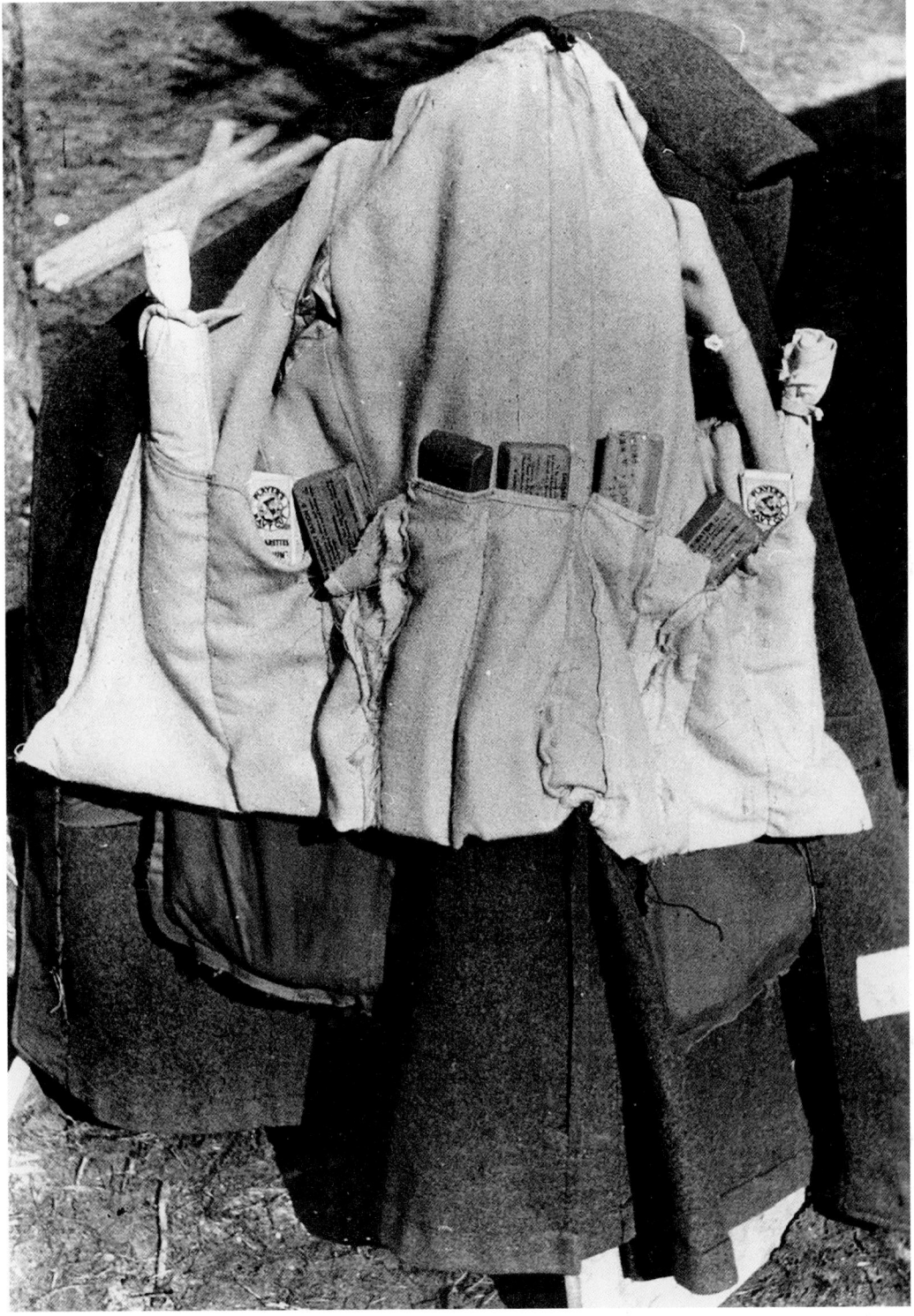

An escape jacket, designed to be worn under normal clothing and having pockets for concentrated food. *(USAFA, SMS 329)*

Showing how compasses were made. A display at a post-war Stalag Luft III reunion. *(USAFA, SMS 329)*

Chapter Eight

Two Famous Escapes

The two escapes which ended in home runs both took place from British compounds. The first was from the East Compound in 1943 and the other from the North Compound the following year.

The Wooden Horse

This was an ingenious plan conceived by three British officers, Flight Lieutenants Oliver Philpot and Eric Williams, and Lieutenant Michael Codner of the Royal Artillery. Codner was one of the few army officers in Stalag Luft III. He had been captured in Tunisia in December 1942 and then taken to Italy and from there mistakenly transferred to Dulag Luft for interrogation by the Luftwaffe. From there he was taken to a POW camp in Poland, where he met Eric Williams. The two made a tunnel escape, but were quickly recaptured and sent to Stalag Luft III. Recognising that the huts, the usual starting point for any tunnel, were a long way from the perimeter fence, and inspired by the story of the Trojan Horse, Codner came up with the idea of constructing a wooden vaulting horse. This could be placed much closer to the wire and used daily by the prisoners for gymnastics. A tunneller would be concealed in the horse and would dig the tunnel, using wooden boards with sand on top to conceal it. The spoil would be put in bags made from trouser pockets and disposed of in the canteen hut. Codner and Williams put the idea to Philpot, who was their hut escape representative. He was very taken with it and they agreed that Philpot could join them. The plan was cleared by the East Compound Escape Committee and work on the tunnel began in July 1943.

The Germans soon got used to the Wooden Horse and the eager vaulters. Initially, Codner and Williams took it in turns to dig, using wash bowls to scoop out the soil. Once the tunnel became long enough, one worked at its face, while the other filled bags with the spoil. These were then collected in a series of trips by another POW, also using the Wooden Horse, which often made two appearances each day. By late October the tunnel was virtually complete. In its final form it ran for some 100ft, with its exit about 15ft beyond the perimeter fence. The 29th of the month was selected as escape day. Codner went down in the early afternoon to make the final preparations, using two air holes to help his breathing. Some two hours later, Williams and

Philpot, together with a third officer of very small stature, were carried out in the Wooden Horse to the tunnel entrance. They joined Codner, while the other officer covered over the entrance before being transported back to the canteen hut, where the horse was kept.

Codner and Williams were to travel together disguised as French draughtsmen, while Philpot, who spoke fluent German, was to masquerade as a Norwegian businessman. All three were dressed in clothes adapted from uniforms and carried small travel bags containing essential toilet items, some concentrated food and additional clothing. They all had numerous forged travel and identity documents. All three planned to reach ports on the Baltic coast and then get on board a Swedish ship. Philpot travelled via Frankfurt-am-Oder, Küstrin (present day Kostrzyn) and Dirschau (Tczew) to Danzig (Gdansk). He was only once asked for his papers on the train and produced his *Ausweis* (Pass), which passed muster even though the photograph on it was not of him. He stayed the night in a hotel in Danzig. He again had to show his papers, which were accepted by the hotelier. Next day he took a ferry round the port and identified a Swedish ship being loaded with coal. He then travelled to the outskirts of Danzig and buried his overcoat and case, leaving him hatless and wearing a dark suit. He took a train back into Danzig and returned to the port. He made his way to the Swedish ship and, evading the guards, decided to board the ship by climbing one of its cables. After one abortive attempt he managed to get on board and found his way to one of the crew's cabins. He was taken to the captain, who said he must leave the ship, since the Germans would be searching it before sailing. There was no attempt to forcibly remove him and so Philpot began to look for somewhere to hide. An officer showed him to a coal bunker. In this way he evaded the German search and the ship sailed at 7.45 the following morning. One of the crew brought him bread and water and late that night he was again taken to see the captain, who now treated him as an honoured guest. The ship docked in Sweden at midnight on 3 November and the following day Philpot was taken to the British Legation in Stockholm. It had been slightly less than a week since he left Stalag Luft III.

It took Codner and Williams somewhat longer to reach Sweden. Their first stop was also Frankfurt-am-Oder, where they spent the first night in a drain, being unable to find beds in a hotel. Unlike Philpot, they opted to take slower stopping trains on the grounds that their papers were less likely to be checked. They caught such a train to Küstrin the following morning, arriving there at midday. After killing time in a restaurant that provided food coupon-free meals and then a cinema, they caught a train to the port of Stettin in the early evening. Again, they were unable to find accommodation for the night and spent it in an air raid shelter in a suburban garden. The next day was a Sunday. They managed to get a hotel room for two nights and then went to explore the docks. They could not get close because of a policeman on the approach bridge and did not spot any Swedish ships. They later drank beer at a number of cafés, hoping to befriend a sympathetic foreign worker, but without success. The following day they went to the docks again and managed to locate a Swedish ship. They hoped to find a Swedish sailor to get them on board. If not, they would find their own way onto the ship. Passing time in a cinema, they returned to the cafés that evening. They did not meet any Swedes, but they went to the docks anyway, only to discover that their ship had sailed. They could find no other Swedish vessel in the dark and decided to return to their hotel. On their way out from the docks they were challenged and showed their *Ausweise*, which seemed to satisfy the guard and they went on their way.

The next morning, they found a sympathetic Frenchman in the docks. He agreed to meet them in his camp that evening and introduce them to a man who spoke English. After filling in more time in the cinema, they got into the camp and met the English speaker, who agreed to pass the word round that they wanted to make contact with Swedish sailors. He agreed to meet them again in two days' time. They had vacated their hotel, but found another one. They were, however, somewhat disconcerted to be sharing the dining room at breakfast next morning with a German colonel and two captains. Another bout of cinema-going and a further virtually fruitless tour of the cafés in the evening took up their fourth day in Stettin. Another change of hotel and the following evening they met the English-speaking Frenchman and another whom they had come across, but neither was of any help. They did eventually meet a French ex-soldier, who said that he was leaving on a ship for Denmark the following night, but did not think that there would be room for Codner and Williams.

Friday 5 November dawned and the escapers were becoming desperate. They were short of food and had run out of hotels to stay in. They decided to return to their original air raid shelter. That evening, before they did so, they met yet another Frenchman, who said that they could sleep in his camp. This they did and finally their luck began to change. Next morning another French contact from another camp came and told them that he had found a Danish sailor who was willing to smuggle them aboard his ship. It was the same one that the French ex-soldier was aboard and they were able to use his pass to enable them to get past the gangway sentry. Their sailor friend hid them in a sail locker and they evaded the routine German search.

First port of call was Copenhagen, which they reached at midday on 7 November. The ship remained there for three days, with Codner and Williams being hidden in a flat on the outskirts. They then sailed on towards Oslo, being hidden for most of the time in the chain locker, which proved very uncomfortable. On 11 November they were taken from the locker to see the first mate, who told them that rather than take them via Oslo to the Swedish port of Gothenburg, which the ship was putting into after Oslo, the idea was that the Swedish pilot, who was on board, would take them with him when he was dropped off at Stromstad, close to the Swedish border with Norway. This duly happened that afternoon and, after a night at the local police station, they were taken to Gothenburg and put in the hands of the British Consul. He arranged for them to travel to Stockholm, where they were reunited with Philpot.

In due course, all three were flown back to Britain and were each awarded the Military Cross. The RAF decided that Philpot and Williams could not return to operational flying. Philpot ended up as a scientific officer in the Air Ministry, while Williams was sent to the Philippines to work with the Americans. In contrast, Codner rejoined the active war, fighting on the Italian Front.

The Great Escape

In contrast to the Wooden Horse, the Great Escape was a much more elaborate affair whose object was to get not just three men but 200 out of the camp. It was very much the brainchild of Big X, Roger Bushell. Up until then, only one tunnel was being dug at a time so that all resources could be concentrated on it. When the Germans discovered it, it meant starting all over again. Bushell therefore reasoned that if a number of tunnels were simultaneously started and the Germans found one, they would relax their guard. He was still in the East Compound at the time, but the North Compound was being constructed. The Germans agreed that some of the POWs could go into the new compound and clear tree stumps, as well as build a new theatre. Bushell took the opportunity to send in some of the mapmakers to carry out a thorough survey of the new compound, and began to plan where the tunnels might be dug. At the same time those involved in digging, carpentry and the other myriad support tasks were organised. This meant that when the North Compound was opened at the end of March 1943, work could begin immediately.

Two tunnels, named Dick and Tom, ran west from the huts. Dick began in a drain in a hut washroom, while Tom's trap was made in the concrete floor of a small annex to one of the barrack rooms. The third tunnel, Harry, ran north from its hut. This made use of a stove standing on tiles. The latter were lifted up and replaced with some from the compound kitchen, which were set in wood so as to provide the trap. It took time to complete the traps and chip away at the concrete underneath, since it was essential that they could not be spotted. From the trap each tunnel had a 30ft shaft with ladders. At the bottom of each shaft three chambers were constructed. One was for the pump which drove the ventilation system. This consisted of pipes made out of Klim cans (Red Cross dried milk, Klim being milk spelt backwards). The second chamber was temporary storage for the spoil, while the third provided storage for tools, shoring, lamps and the like. During the hours of darkness the tunnels were lit by electric light tapped off the camp system. The latter was, however, switched off during the day and so lamps filled with margarine had to be used. Diggers were taken up the tunnels and spoil brought back using trolleys on wooden rails. To get rid of the spoil, the main method used was for prisoners to suspend bags underneath their clothing and then scatter the sand in various parts of the compound, scuffing up the ground so that it would not become too obvious. It was all a far cry from the Wooden Horse.

In spite of serious falls of sand in both Dick and Harry, work progressed well on all three tunnels. In July 1943 it was decided to concentrate on Tom because the Germans were building a new compound (West) where its exit would be. Dick was to be used for the dispersal of soil. Tom proceeded well. By 10 October it had reached a length of 285ft, but on that day a Ferret idly tapping the site of the trap with a pickaxe dislodged a chip from it. Tom was therefore discovered. The Germans partially blew it up and it was abandoned. Harry was immediately reopened, but closed a week later, since winter was now approaching. This would have added fresh and unnecessary obstacles for escapers, especially the frost and snow, and so it was better to delay the escape until the onset of spring. It was reopened in January 1944 and, after some maintenance work, digging recommenced. The spoil was now taken to the compound theatre and hidden under its floor. At the beginning of March there was a blow, when the chief engineer of Harry, and others working on it, were transferred to the satellite camp of Belaria, which had opened in January 1944, but operations continued and by mid-March Harry had reached the required length of 245ft. The last 50ft of rail needed to have the noise muffled, which was done using blankets. The trolleys now had to be filled in with wood so they could be used to take a prone escaper up the tunnel. Stronger ropes were thus needed. They were acquired from materials for a boxing ring the Germans intended to construct.

Meanwhile, the escapers themselves had been preparing. A major reason why Bushell wanted to spring so many was to cause maximum embarrassment to the Germans. As to his selection of the 200, this was made two weeks before the actual escape. Those who had been actively involved with the tunnels were the priority, as were experienced escapers, who were invariably also in the first category. Men from Occupied Europe who were flying with the RAF were another priority on the grounds that they could more easily pass themselves off as foreign workers. The first thirty escapers were travelling by train and were issued with just a small map of the frontier they planned to cross and the necessary documents. They were not given Red Cross food and general maps, since these would make them vulnerable if searched. They also had small cases, which had been acquired by prisoners when at another camp. Forty others would travel by workmen's stopping trains for part of their journey, while the remainder were to travel on foot. Even though the number of men being issued with full papers was limited, it still put enormous pressure on the forgers, tailors, mapmakers and others. At the same time security remained paramount, both in terms of monitoring the movements of the Germans and concealing the growing collection of escape equipment.

The night of 24/25 March 1944 was chosen for the escape to be made, since there would be no moon. The escapers gathered that night in Hut 104, from where Harry originated. Tunnellers who were not escapers acted as trolley haulers. When the exit was opened at 10.15pm, it was discovered that it was 15ft short of the trees; the surveyors had miscalculated. Bushell, who was at the bottom of the exit shaft, decided that the escapers would operate in parties of ten. The first man out would take with him a rope, one end of which was attached to the exit ladder. He would tie the other end to a tree. Each man as he exited would keep one hand on the rope, which could be jerked to warn him to lie flat and keep still in the event of searchlights or German patrols in the area. Once each man had reached the treeline, the rope would be tugged as a signal for the next man to exit. This, however, meant a delay in the timings.

The first escaper entered the trap at 10.30pm. He was hauled in a succession of three trolleys to the exit and then made his way out. The initial thirty escapers took longer to get out than expected, and the electricity being turned off because of a nearby air raid did not help. The next batch were carrying blankets containing their food and other items. In many cases the blankets had not been rolled tightly enough to clear the ceiling and sides of the tunnel. The order was therefore made for no more blanket rolls to be taken. Two falls of sand also slowed progress. The last escape was scheduled for 5.00am and ten minutes earlier it was decided that the eighty-sixth escaper would be the last. Just as he went down through the trap there was a rifle shot. The seven escapers in the tunnel were recalled and the trap and stove replaced.

At the exit end of Harry, the Germans had spotted what was happening and arrested three of the escapers on the spot. Of the other seventy-six, some were arrested close to Sagan, but others managed to get further afield before being caught. One POW made it to Czechoslovakia and remained there in hiding until November 1944. The truth was that the Germans realised very quickly that there had been a mass escape and a widespread alert was put out. Hitler soon got to hear of it and was furious. He initially wanted all those captured to be shot, but this was reduced to a list of fifty, including Roger Bushell, who was, in any event, a marked man. All of those who were to be murdered were handed over to the Gestapo and, wherever they were held, they were taken in cars on the pretext of being sent back to a camp. During the journey the car would stop and the prisoner would be told to get out to relieve himself. He would then be shot in the back of the head by one of the Gestapo men.

Yet amid all this tragedy, three of the escapers, two Norwegians and a Dutchman, made home runs. The Norwegians, Sergeant Per Bergsland and Lieutenant Jens Muller, decided to travel together. Like the Wooden Horse trio, they planned to get to Stettin and then find a Swedish ship. Their cover was that they were Norwegian electricians from a camp at Frankfurt-am-Oder who had been doing a job near Sagan. This would enable them to travel back to Frankfurt. They also had letters ordering them to report to an office in Stettin. Their rail journeys went smoothly, with their papers standing up to inspection at Küstrin, and they arrived at Stettin at 1.00pm on 25 March. They killed time until dusk, when they went to a French brothel, whose address they had been given by the Escape Organisation. They came across a Swedish sailor, who took them to the docks. They went to where his ship was anchored and he said he would give them a signal when it was safe to come aboard. They saw the ship sail, although no signal had been given, and so returned to the town and stayed the remainder of the night and most of the next day in a hotel room. They returned to the brothel that evening and met two more Swedish sailors coming out. Their ship was berthed 3 miles away and so the sailors took Bergsland and Muller there by train. They closely followed the two Swedes up the gangway, the German guard not bothering to ask for their papers. They were hidden in the anchor chain locker and sailed at 7.00am on 28 March, reaching Gothenburg late the following day.

Flight Lieutenant Bram Vanderstok elected to go via his native Holland and then down into France, where he hoped to be passed by an escape line into Spain. He initially had some anxious moments. In the woods outside the camp he was accosted by a German civilian. Vanderstok explained that he was a Dutch worker and was scared that the police might arrest him for being out during an air raid – there was one taking place over Berlin. The German swallowed the story and insisted on escorting him to Sagan railway station. There he noticed one of the female censors from the camp, who expressed her suspicions about him and another escaper. She got a German officer to inspect their papers, but they were accepted. Thereafter Vanderstok's rail journey to Holland went relatively smoothly, although he was asked for his papers several times. He dared not go near his family for fear they were being watched by the Gestapo and ended up in Utrecht, where he had attended university. He made contact with two of his professors, one of whom took him in for the night. Thereafter, he was put in the hands of the Dutch Underground and stayed in a series of safe houses. The Underground saw him across the River Maas and into Belgium. He had an uncle who was the director of an Antwerp shipyard and through his good offices Vanderstok managed to obtain Belgian money and a safe house in Brussels. A Dutch family lived there, the father being involved with the Belgian Underground.

After three weeks with nothing happening, Vanderstok decided to make his own way to Paris. His uncle had arranged for him to have some French francs and his host in Brussels procured for him a permit which allowed Belgian workers to commute to Valenciennes across the border. The Underground also arranged for him to meet a certain Frenchman at a certain time and place in Paris. Unfortunately, Vanderstok's train took an age to reach Paris and arrived too late for him to make the rendezvous in time. He went to the meeting place at the appointed time the following day, but there was no sign of his contact. He therefore decided to take a train to Toulouse, substituting his new destination for Paris on his travel permit. He was going to Toulouse because his Belgian contact had given him the name of a café in a small town just beyond Toulouse where he would be put in touch with the escape line. He duly arrived at the café in the early afternoon of 10 May 1944. The family that owned it were members of the Maquis. After two days Vanderstok was taken to a farmhouse 20 miles away. There he joined a party which included other Allied airmen and some German Jews.

That night the party set off for Spain accompanied by a guide and two other Maquis men. Shortly after dawn they halted, with the foothills of the Pyrenees in sight. The guide, accompanied by Vanderstok and another man, went to obtain bread from a small village. Leaving the two escapers under cover, the guide went to a café to collect the food. At that moment a German patrol appeared and the guide was killed. Vanderstok and his companion returned to the main group, but they already knew what had happened. They slaughtered a sheep and ate it boiled. That night they were taken to a ruined castle, which the Maquis used as a stronghold. There they were given bread and water and introduced to a new guide. Three nights' march took them to within sight of Spain. They were now on their own, but made it across the border and into the hands of Spanish soldiers. Eventually, Vanderstok made contact with the British Consul in Lerida and went by train via Madrid to Gibraltar, which he reached on 8 July 1944. Before he flew back to Britain, he arranged for postcards to be sent from Spain to a fellow Dutchman in Stalag Luft III to indicate that he had made a home run.

(**Left**) Michael Codner. After the war he joined the Colonial Service and was posted as a District Officer to Malaya, where he was born. He was killed in 1952 in a Communist terrorist ambush. (*Michael Codner*)

(**Centre**) Oliver Philpot. He had already won a DFC, when he was shot down flying a Beaufort on an anti-shipping sortie. He became a very successful businessman after the war. (*Robert J. Laplander*)

(**Right**) Eric Williams wrote two books about his escape experiences: *The Tunnel*, which related the escape that he and Michael Codner carried out from Stalag Luft I and the better known *The Wooden Horse*, which was made into a feature film. (*Robert J. Laplander*)

A replica of the Wooden Horse. The original was made, as was so much else in the camp, from Red Cross boxes. The carrying handles were slid out when the box was being used for vaulting. *(Robert J. Laplander)*

Codner's forged temporary pass allowing him to be away from his normal place of work in Breslau. *(Michael Codner)*

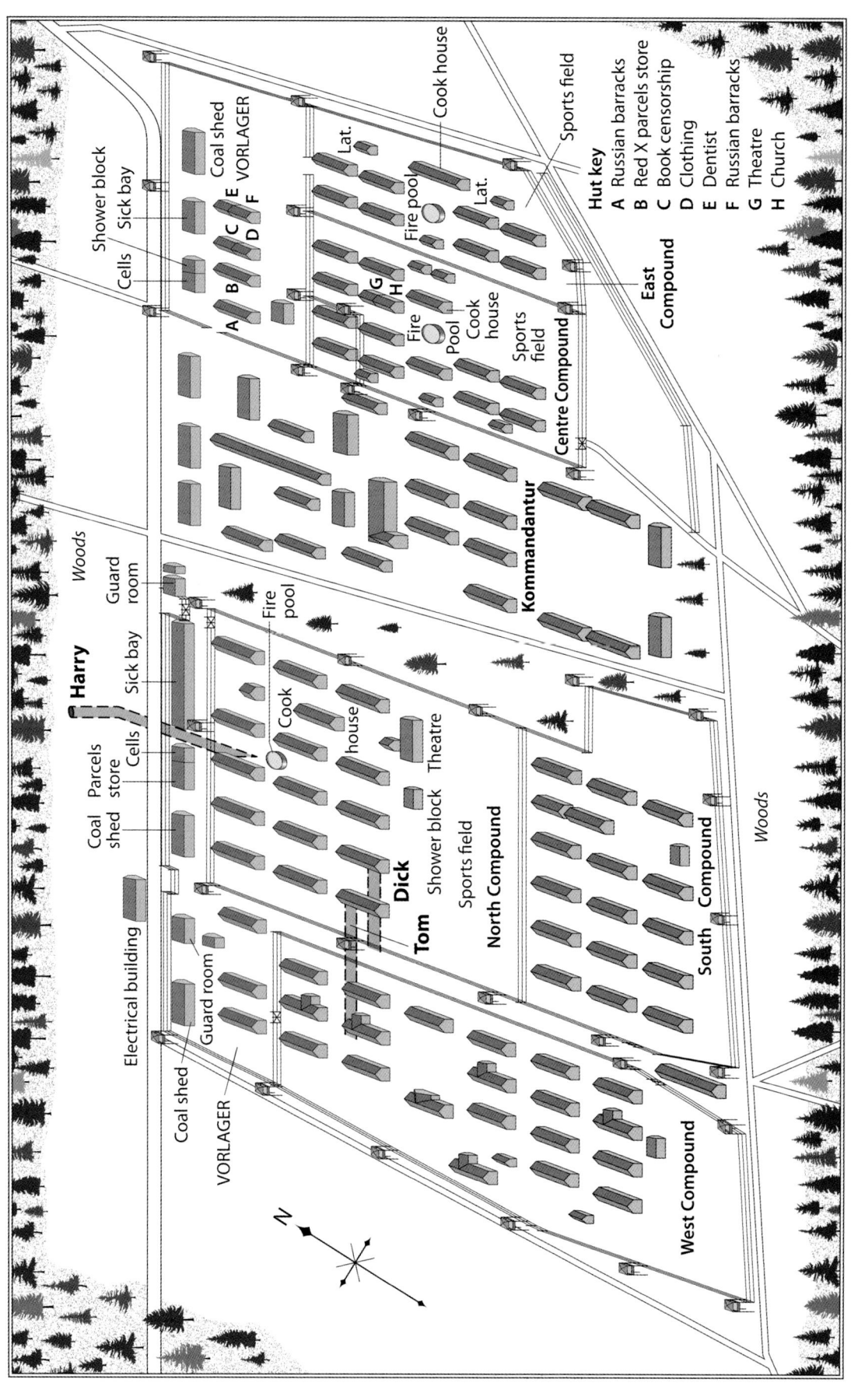

Stalag Luft III in its final form, but showing the Tom, Dick and Harry tunnels in the North Compound.

Digging Harry.

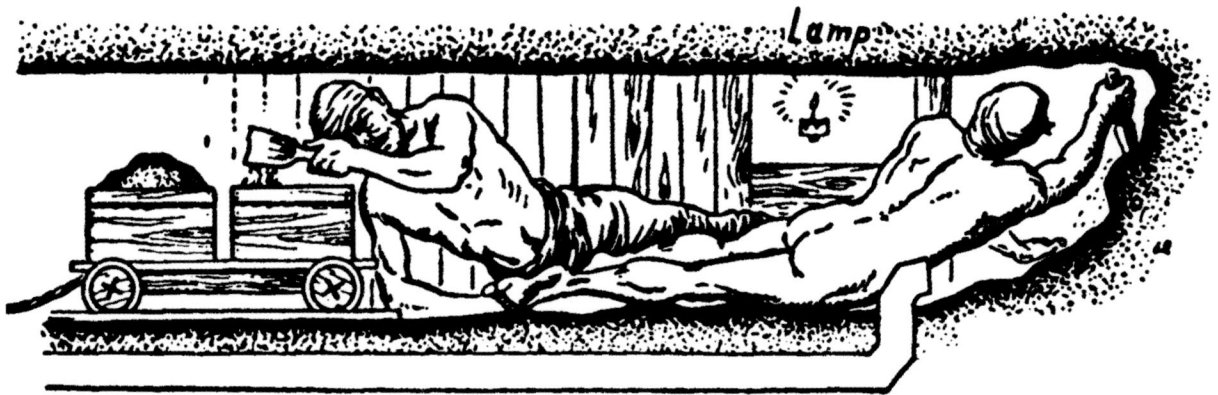

Harry in its final form. Note the three compartments at the bottom of the entrance and the two places along the tunnel where the escapers exchanged trolleys. (*Luka Cyrian*)

Harry's entrance shaft with ladder. (USAFA, SMS 329)

Inside Harry. (*USAFA, SMS 329*)

A trolley from Harry. Trolleys were a great improvement on the sledges used in previous tunnels. (*USAFA, SMS 329*)

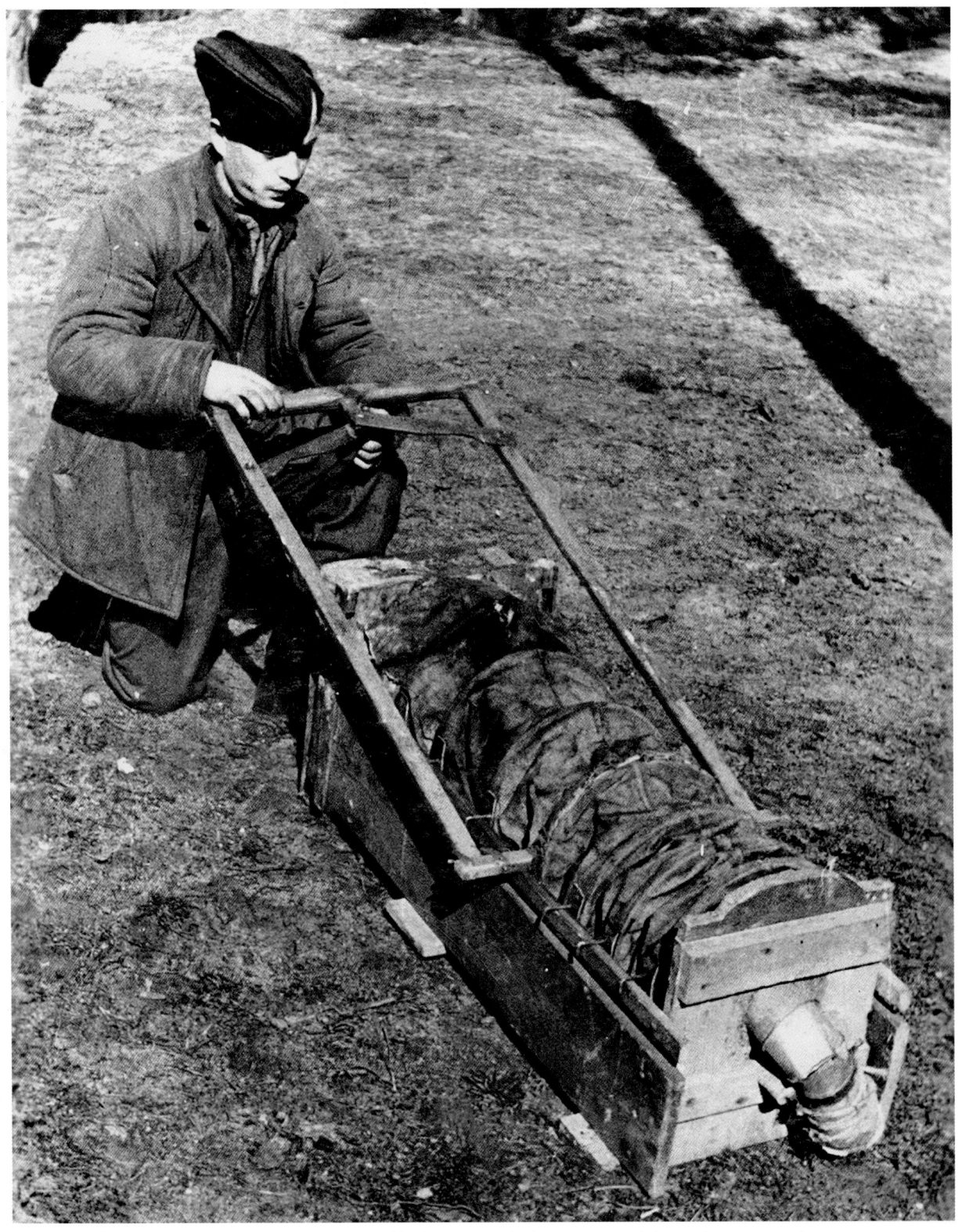
Harry's air pump. It was made from a kitbag, with the springs being converted from chest expanders. (*USAFA, SMS 329*)

(**Above**) Harry's exit, showing the rope that was used to alert the next escaper that he could set off for the tree line, using the rope to guide him. (**Below**) A Ferret on the exit ladder. (*USAFA, SMS 329*)

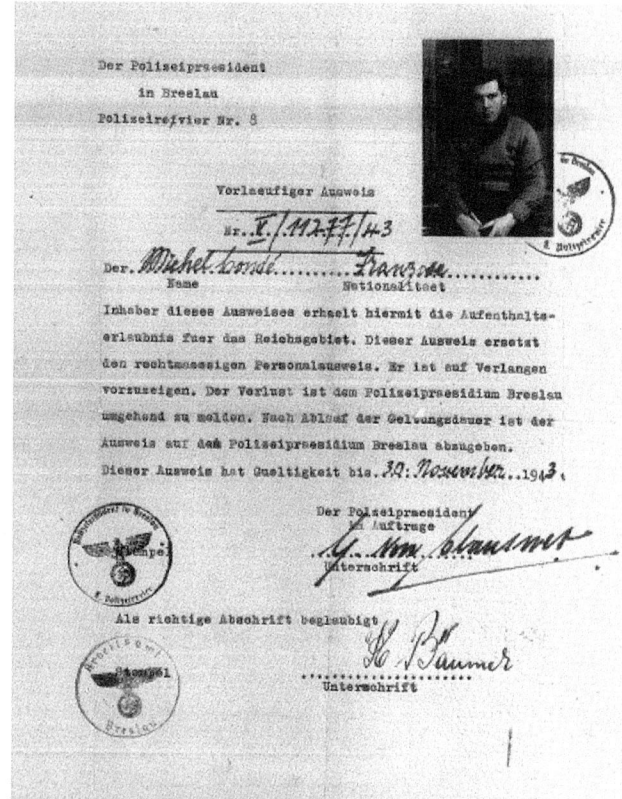

Eric Williams' forged temporary pass. Compare it with that of Codner and one can see the quality of the forging
(Robert J. Laplander)

Three intrepid Norwegians: Per Bergsland (*left*) and Jen Muller (*right*) made successful home runs during the Great Escape. Haldor Espelid (*centre*) was not so lucky. He was arrested in Flensburg and murdered on 29 March 1944.
(Jonathan Vance)

Bram (also known as Bob) Vanderstok finished the war commanding 322 (Dutch) Squadron RAF and was Holland's most highly decorated airman. He returned to his medical studies after the war and moved to the USA, finishing up in Hawaii. *(Bram Vanderstok)*

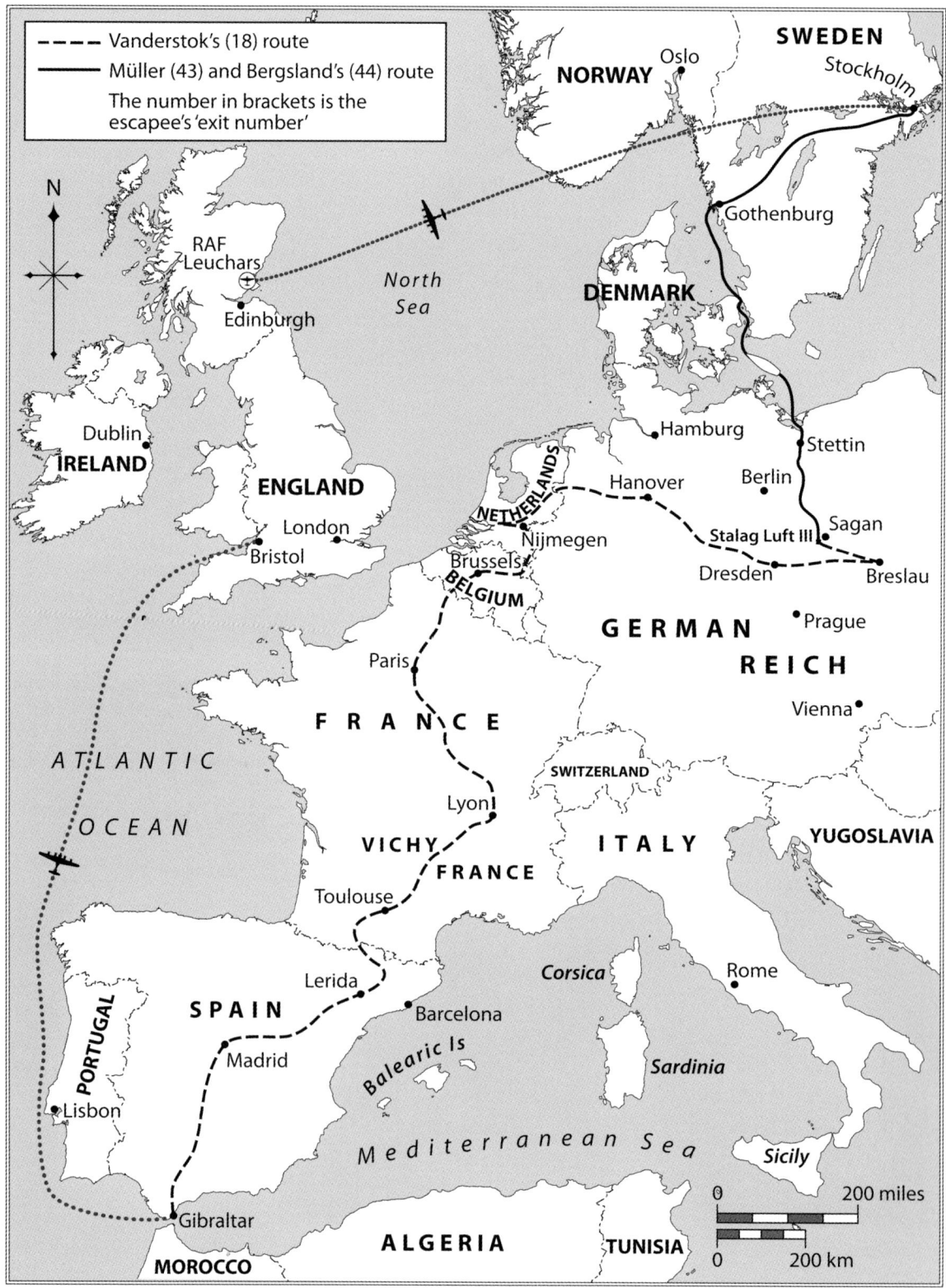

The escape routes taken by Bergsland, Muller and Vanderstok.

Vanderstok's train ticket from Breslau to Alkmaar. *(Bram Vanderstok)*

Chapter Nine

Great Escape Aftermath

In the immediate aftermath of the Great Escape, the remaining occupants of Hut 104 were made to find accommodation elsewhere, while the Germans investigated Harry. Curiously, they did not search the hut and so a lot of escape equipment was preserved. The first effects of Hitler's anger were felt on 26 March when von Lindeiner was removed from command and replaced by another Luftwaffe officer, Colonel Korda. However, Heinrich Himmler's Gestapo had long wanted to take control of the POW camps and the Great Escape gave them the ideal pretext. The first indication of this was when the Gestapo carried out the investigation into how the mass escape from Stalag Luft III had been allowed to happen.

Then some of those escapers who had avoided death at the hands of the Gestapo began to return to the camp, each being sentenced to twenty-one days in the Cooler. A few others, including 'Wings' Day, were sent to Sachsenhausen concentration camp, their fate uncertain. There was, though, growing concern over what had happened to the majority of the escapers. This was clarified on 6 April when Group Captain Massey, the Senior British Officer in the North Compound, was summoned to the Commandant's officer with an interpreter. Colonel Korda read from a report which stated that forty-one of the escapers had been shot while resisting arrest or attempting further escape. Massey asked how many had been wounded and the answer was none. He then asked for the names of the victims and for their remains to be returned for burial. Returning to the compound, Massey informed the hut leaders. A few days later a list of forty-seven names was published, to which three more were later added. A short time afterwards fifty cremation urns arrived and the prisoners were allowed to erect a memorial in the woods outside the camp.

The murders came as an enormous shock to the prisoners. They realised that escaping now bore additional grave risks. But there was also anger that the Germans could have committed such an atrocity. Indeed, from then on relations between prisoners and captors chilled. It so happened that shortly afterwards Group Captain Massey was repatriated back to Britain because of his wounds and he immediately alerted the authorities as to what had happened. The RAF set in train an investigation and Foreign Minister Anthony Eden made statements in the House of Commons making it clear that the government was certain the fifty men had been murdered.

Besides the deterrent effect of the Great Escape killings, there was another reason why there was less inclination to prepare escapes. Germany was increasingly staring defeat in the face, especially after the successful Normandy landings and the Russian offensive in the summer of 1944, Operation Bagration, which drove the Germans back across the River Vistula. There was, too, the increasing intensity of the Anglo–American 'round the clock' bombing. Indeed, in September 1944 MI9 issued an edict that British officers should no longer consider it their duty to escape. The Americans received similar instructions. Even so, another tunnel, George, was started in the North Compound that summer; it was, however, closed in the autumn. Fears now grew that, given the ever-more desperate situation that the Nazis found themselves in, they might be tempted to murder the POWs. Consequently, the plan now was that if this appeared likely, the prisoners would manufacture their own weapons to use against the guards and stockpile them in George, which remained undiscovered.

By the beginning of 1945 Stalag Luft III contained over 15,000 POWs. The German ration had been reduced, but the Red Cross parcels were still getting through. The war, though, was on the move. The Americans had recovered from the German assault in the Ardennes and were advancing once more. On the Eastern Front the Russians opened their long-awaited offensive which would take them from the Vistula to the Oder. In Stalag Luft III they heard of POW camps further east being evacuated in the face of the rapid Russian advance. Refugees were seen passing the camp. The prisoners therefore began to prepare for evacuation. Sledges were made and the contents of Red Cross parcels packed. On Sunday, 27 January the Commandant was told that there would be no evacuation. That evening the order was countermanded and the prisoners were told that they were to move out in one hour's time. There was deep snow on the ground and it was dark. The inmates of the South Compound were first to leave and it was vacated by 11.00pm. Other compounds followed, with the inmates of the North Compound leaving Hut 104, of Great Escape fame, mysteriously in flames. The Belaria POWs did not leave until the following evening.

The columns set out accompanied by their guards. Apart from the cold, accommodation was the main problem. The Germans, too, had provided little in the way of food. Many of the villages that they passed through had little to offer. The prisoners sometimes had to make marches well in excess of the 20km maximum laid down by the Geneva Conventions. Yet in spite of the fact that refugees from the east had already passed this way, the local inhabitants gave what help they could. The POWs eventually arrived at Spremberg, some 40 miles due west of Sagan, after a week on the road. From there the columns went by rail to a number of destinations. Those from the North Compound, with some from the East, were sent to a POW camp which had been for naval personnel and lay between Bremen and Hamburg. Those from Belaria and the balance from the East Compound ended up at a camp 20 miles south-west of Berlin. The American compounds were also split. POWs from the

West Compound were sent to a camp near Nuremberg, while those from the South and Centre Compounds had a camp at Moosburg, north-east of Munich, as their destination. The rail journeys were, however, as uncomfortable as the marches. The POWs were crammed into freight wagons, so tightly that it was impossible for all them to sit or lie down. The conditions were aggravated by the fact that some of the wagons had had cattle as their previous cargo. There was also the threat of being strafed by marauding Allied aircraft.

The camps that the prisoners eventually arrived at were generally overcrowded anyway. The Nuremberg camp was also close to a marshalling yard which was a frequent target for American planes. Indeed, some POWs became casualties of the bombing and a formal complaint was lodged with the Protecting Power that the camp was sited too close to a military target. Food was also meagre and the supply of Red Cross parcels seemed to have dried up. This was the same at all the camps. There were also rumours that the prisoners would be moved to the so-called Alpine Redoubt and used as bargaining counters (as happened to the few Stalag Luft III escapers who were sent to Sachsenhausen).

Behind the scenes there were developments. Brigadier General Arthur W. Vanaman, the senior American officer at Stalag Luft III, and Colonel Delmar T. Spivey, who had been in charge of the East Compound, were removed from the columns at Spremberg, together with three other officers, and taken to Berlin. There they were to meet Waffen SS General Gottlieb Berger, who had been placed in charge of Allied POWs. After much waiting around, they were made to attend a medical conference in late March designed to improve the conditions of the prisoners. Eventually, Berger met them on the evening of 3 April. He wanted them to carry radio codes to the Western Allies so that a separate peace could be negotiated, a plan that a number of high-ranking Nazis were individually pursuing. They agreed to travel to Switzerland to execute this. In return, they asked Berger to guarantee the flow of Red Cross parcels, which he did. Hitler's idea of moving large numbers of prisoners to the Alpine Redoubt came to nothing. Instead, the POWs at Nuremberg were moved in early April to Moosburg, which aggravated the overcrowding still further. At much the same time the British POWs began to move east towards Lübeck from their camp between Bremen and Hamburg.

It was now just a matter of time before the prisoners were liberated. Fearing that they might get caught up in the fighting, some Americans at Moosburg slipped out of the camp and hid themselves in the town. Finally, on Sunday 29 April the liberators arrived at Moosburg. A P-51 Mustang flew low over the camp. Guards in one of the Goon towers fired at it and the plane retaliated, destroying the watchtower. There was a brief firefight involving SS elements and then an American tank crashed through the camp's perimeter fence. The British to the north had to wait a little longer, until 2 May, for liberation.

Curiously, at Moosburg it was Group Captain Willetts, the former SBO of East Compound, who took the surrender as the senior Allied officer present. It is not clear what he was doing there. The German who surrendered to him was none other than Major Gustav Simoleit, the Second-in-Command at Stalag Luft III. He had led the original march to Moosburg and found himself in charge of the camp. Warrant Officer Hermann Glemnitz was also at the camp. Both became prisoners themselves and endured a hard time in immediate post-war Germany. Such had been their conduct, though, that they subsequently attended a number of Stalag Luft III reunions. As for Friedrich von Lindeiner, the former commandant of the camp, he was told that he would face a court martial, together with ten members of the camp staff, for allowing the Great Escape to happen. He retired to his home to work out his defence, but when it was announced that the court martial would be held in September 1944 in Berlin, von Lindeiner's friends arranged for him to be admitted to a local hospital on the grounds of mental illness. He was therefore never prosecuted. The hospital moved west when the Russians approached, but von Lindeiner was discharged just as this was about to happen. He joined in the defence of the Sagan area. He was wounded and evacuated westwards, ending up as a prisoner of the British.

At the end of the war there was one piece of unfinished business as far as Stalag Luft III was concerned: the pursuit of the Gestapo men who had murdered the fifty escapers. A team from the RAF's Special Investigation Branch flew out to Germany in the summer of 1945 to identify and track them down. They had already been investigating among German prisoners in Britain. The team managed to identify the murderers of all but six of the escapers. In many cases the Gestapo men had shot more than one prisoner. The first of two trials was conducted at Hamburg in July 1947. There were eighteen defendants, all of whom were found guilty. Thirteen were sentenced to death by hanging and the remainder given varying terms of imprisonment. In September 1948, however, the British government announced that it was ceasing to pursue war crimes. This meant that five arrested Gestapo men were not charged and had to be freed. A further trial of three men did take place in Hamburg that October. Two were found guilty of murder and sentenced to death, but in both cases this was reduced to a life sentence. In summary, seventy-two Germans had been identified as being implicated in the murders, of whom twenty-six had been tracked down by the RAF. Others were executed by the Russians and Czechs for other war crimes, while a few had committed suicide. The remainder could not be traced. Even so, the Great Escape victims did obtain some justice.

(**Opposite, above**) Four of the Great Escape's participants photographed by the German police immediately after their capture in Flensburg, Schleswig-Holstein. They are still wearing their escape clothes. (*Left to right*): Haldor Espelid, Nils Fuglesang, James Catanach DFC and Arnold Christensen. They were shot that same day, 29 March 1944, by Gestapo man Johannes Post, who was later hanged for his crimes, as were others involved.

(**Opposite, below**) Part of the memorial made by the POWs to honour the fifty men who lost their lives in the Great Escape. (*USAFA, SMS 329*)

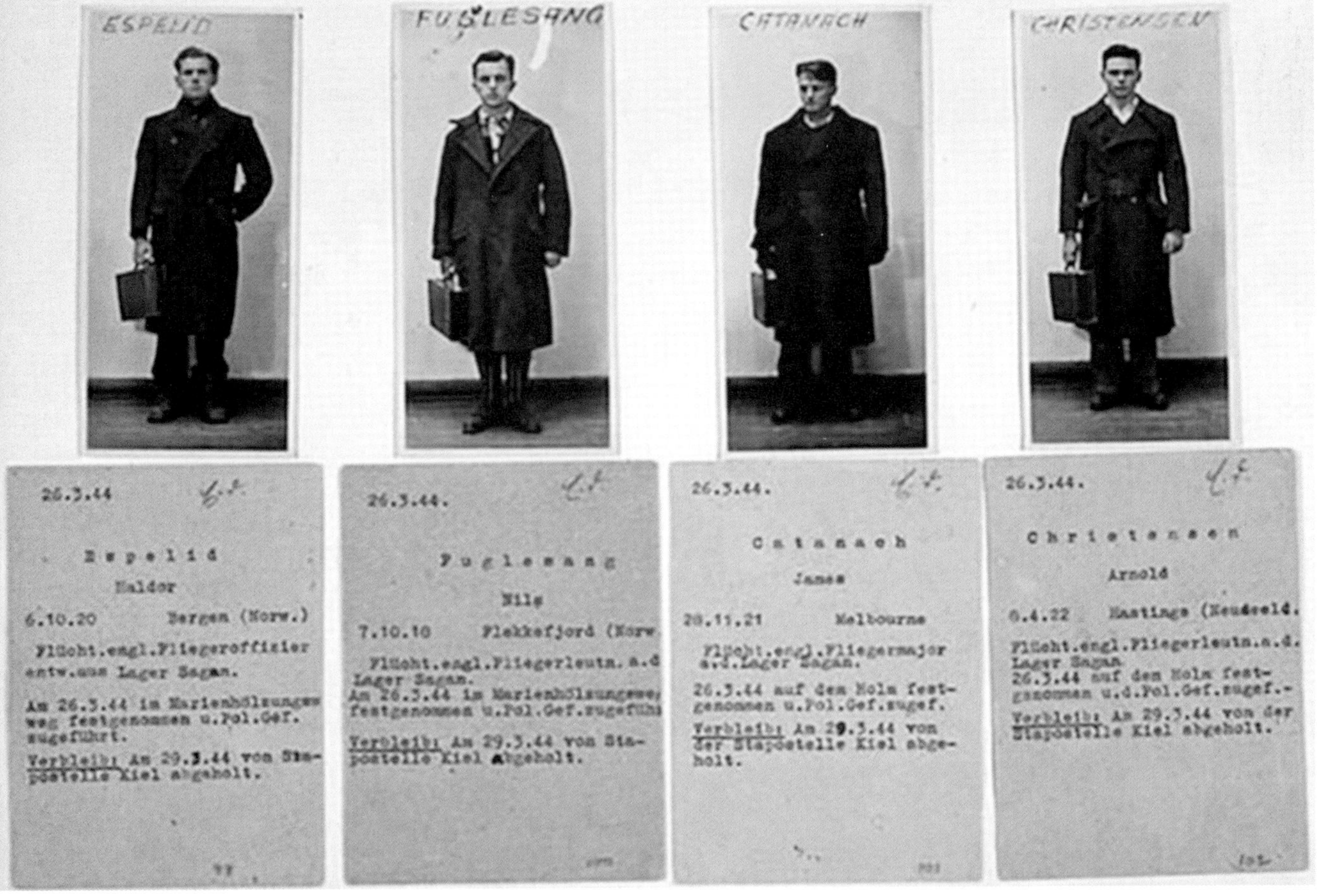

```
26.3.44.                    26.3.44.                    26.3.44.                    26.3.44.

  Espelid                     Fuglesang                   Catanach                    Christensen
    Haldor                       Nils                       James                       Arnold
6.10.20   Bergen (Norw.)     7.10.18  Flekkefjord (Norw.) 28.11.21   Melbourne        8.4.22  Hastings (Neuseeld.)
Flücht.engl.Fliegeroffizier  Flücht.engl.Fliegerleutn.a.d. Flücht.engl.Fliegermajor  Flücht.engl.Fliegerleutn.a.d.
entw.aus Lager Sagan.        Lager Sagan.                 a.d. Lager Sagan.           Lager Sagan.
Am 26.3.44 im Marienhölzungs-Am 26.3.44 im Marienhölzungs-26.3.44 auf dem Holm fest-  26.3.44 auf dem Holm fest-
weg festgenommen u.Pol.Gef.  weg festgenommen u.Pol.Gef.  genommen u.d.Pol.Gef.zugef. genommen u.d.Pol.Gef.zugef.-
zugeführt.                   zugeführt.                   Verbleib: Am 29.3.44 von     Verbleib: Am 29.3.44 von der
Verbleib: Am 29.3.44 von Sta-Verbleib: Am 29.3.44 von Sta-der Stapostelle Kiel abge-   Stapostelle Kiel abgeholt.
postelle Kiel abgeholt.      postelle Kiel abgeholt.      holt.
```

F/O PICARD H.A.	F/L STREET D.O.	F/L HALL CH.P.	F/L LEIGH T.B.
F/O POHE J.	F/O TOBOLSKI P.	F/L HUMPHRIES E.S.	F/L LONG J.L.R.
F/L SCHEIDHAUER B.	F/O VALENTA G.W.	F/O KIDDER G.A.	F/L McGARR C.A.N.
F/O SKANZIKLAS S.	F/L WALENN E.	F/O KIERATH R.V.	F/L McGILL G.E.
F/L SWAIN E.O.	F/L WERNHAM J.C.	F/L KIEWNARSKI A.	F/L MARCINKUS R.
F/L STEVENS R.J.	F/L MILLEY G.W.	S/L KIRBY GREEN T.G.	F/L MILFORD H.J.
F/O STOWER J.B.	F/L WILLIAMS J.E.	F/O KOLANOWSKI W.	F/O MONDSCHEIN J.
F/O STEWART R.G.	F/L WILLIAMS J.F.	F/O KRÓL S.Z.	F/L PAWLUK K.
		F/L LANGFORD P.	

To all Prisoners of War!

The escape from prison camps is no longer a sport!

Germany has always kept to the Hague Convention and only punished recaptured prisoners of war with minor disciplinary punishment.

Germany will still maintain these principles of international law.

But England has besides fighting at the front in an honest manner instituted an illegal warfare in non combat zones in the form of gangster commandos, terror bandits and sabotage troops even up to the frontiers of Germany.

They say in a captured secret and confidential English military pamphlet,

THE HANDBOOK OF MODERN IRREGULAR WARFARE:

". . . the days when we could practise the rules of sportsmanship are over. For the time being, every soldier must be a potential gangster and must be prepared to adopt their methods whenever necessary."

"The sphere of operations should always include the enemy's own country, any occupied territory, and in certain circumstances, such neutral countries as he is using as a source of supply."

England has with these instructions opened up a non military form of gangster war!

Germany is determined to safeguard her homeland, and especially her war industry and provisional centres for the fighting fronts. Therefore it has become necessary to create strictly forbidden zones, called death zones, in which all unauthorised trespassers will be immediately shot on sight.

Escaping prisoners of war, entering such death zones, will certainly lose their lives. They are therefore in constant danger of being mistaken for enemy agents or sabotage groups.

<u>Urgent warning is given against making future escapes!</u>

In plain English: Stay in the camp where you will be safe! Breaking out of it is now a damned dangerous act.

<u>The chances of preserving your life are almost nil!</u>

All police and military guards have been given the most strict orders to shoot on sight all suspected persons.

Escaping from prison camps has ceased to be a sport!

In 1944, after the Great Escape, the Germans issued several posters like this. (USAFA, SMS 25)

US bombing raid close to Stalag Luft III. These became more frequent as 1944 wore on. *(USAFA, SMS 757)*

The increasing Allied air raids in the area during 1944 caused slit trenches to be dug as a precaution against the camp being inadvertently bombed. *(USAFA, SMS 329)*

(**Above & facing**) Three photographs taken on the Long March, January 1945. (USAFA, SMS 329)

Another shot of the Long March. A thaw soon set in, which meant that the sledges the POWs had made were no longer viable. *(USAFA, SMS 329)*

A half-completed hut at the camp of Nuremberg to which some Stalag Luft III prisoners were taken after the Long March. *(USAFA, SMS 329)*

The problem with the Nuremberg camp was that it was too close to the marshalling yards, which were subject to frequent US bombing attacks, as shown here. *(USAFA, SMS 329)*

POWs arriving at the Nuremberg camp. *(USAFA, SMS 329)*

(**Right**) Gottlieb Berger, who took over control of the POW camps in Germany in July 1944 and summoned General Vanaman and Colonel Spivey to Berlin during the Long March. He was later imprisoned for over six years for war crimes. (USAFA, SMS 329)

(**Below**) Stammlager VIIA Moosburg, where most of the US prisoners from Stalag Luft III finished their war. The tents were an effort to ease the overcrowding. (USAFA, SMS 329)

(**Opposite, above**) A convoy of Red Cross trucks from Switzerland and carrying Red Cross parcels arrives at Moosburg. SS General Gottlieb Berger had been instrumental in arranging this. (USAFA, SMS 329)

(**Opposite, below**) Improvised cooking at Moosburg: another indication of the overcrowding. (USAFA, SMS 329)

A strongpoint inside the camp at Moosburg. It was a grim indication that fighting might well take place there. As it was, the SS detachments defending the town offered only token resistance, although certainly one US tank round did penetrate one of the camp buildings. (USAFA, SMS 329)

The surrender of Moosburg, 29 April 1945. (Left to right): Major Gustav Simoleit, Lieutenant Colonel James W. Lann, commanding the 47th Tank Battalion, which liberated the camp, Group Captain Albert Willett. (USAFA, SMS 329)

One of the Sherman tanks which liberated the camp at Moosburg. (*USAFA, SMS 329*)

Freedom at last for the Moosburg POWs, including many from Stalag Luft III. (*USAFA, SMS 329*)

General George S. Patton, commander US Third Army, visited the camp at Moosburg the day after its liberation. Group Captain Willetts is in attendance. (USAFA, SMS 329)

American POWs waiting to board C-47 transports on the first leg of their journey home. RAF Bomber Command flew many of the British prisoners back to Britain. (USAFA, SMS 329)

Home at last. The Statue of Liberty, as seen from a ship carrying former Stalag Luft III American POWs, 3 June 1945. (*USAFA, SMS 329*)

Squadron Leader Frank McKenna of the RAF's Special Investigation Branch arresting Erich Zacharias in the Bremen docks. Zacharias would be found guilty of involvement in the murders of Flying Officer Kidder and Squadron Leader Kirby-Green in Czechoslakia on 29 March 1944 and was subsequently hanged.

A Stalag Luft III Kriegie reunion in the USA. (USAFA, SMS 329)

Chapter Ten

The Camp Today

Stalag Luft III no longer exists, but there is a museum in its place. This was originally opened in 1971 as the Museum of Allied Prisoners of War Martyrdom, but its name was changed in 2009 to the POW Camps Museum. It commemorates all the POW camps in the Zagan area and contains a number of artefacts from them, as well as re-creations of aspects of Stalag Luft III, including a typical living room in one of the huts, the perimeter fence and a Goon Box. The Museum also hosts a number of annual commemorative events.

POW Camps Museum, Zagan. (*POW Camps Museum*)

(**Above**) Replica of a Goon Box. *(POW Camps Museum)*

(**Opposite, above**) Replica of a Stalag Luft III barrack room. Note the Klim dried milk cans on the table. These provided the ducting for the Great Escape tunnel's ventilation. *(POW Camps Museum)*

(**Opposite, below**) Recreation of another Stalag Luft III barrack room. The Red Cross food parcels included powdered milk in tin cans that were refashioned into candle holders and scoops. *(Luka Cyprian)*

(**Below**) Replica barrack hut. *(POW Camps Museum)*

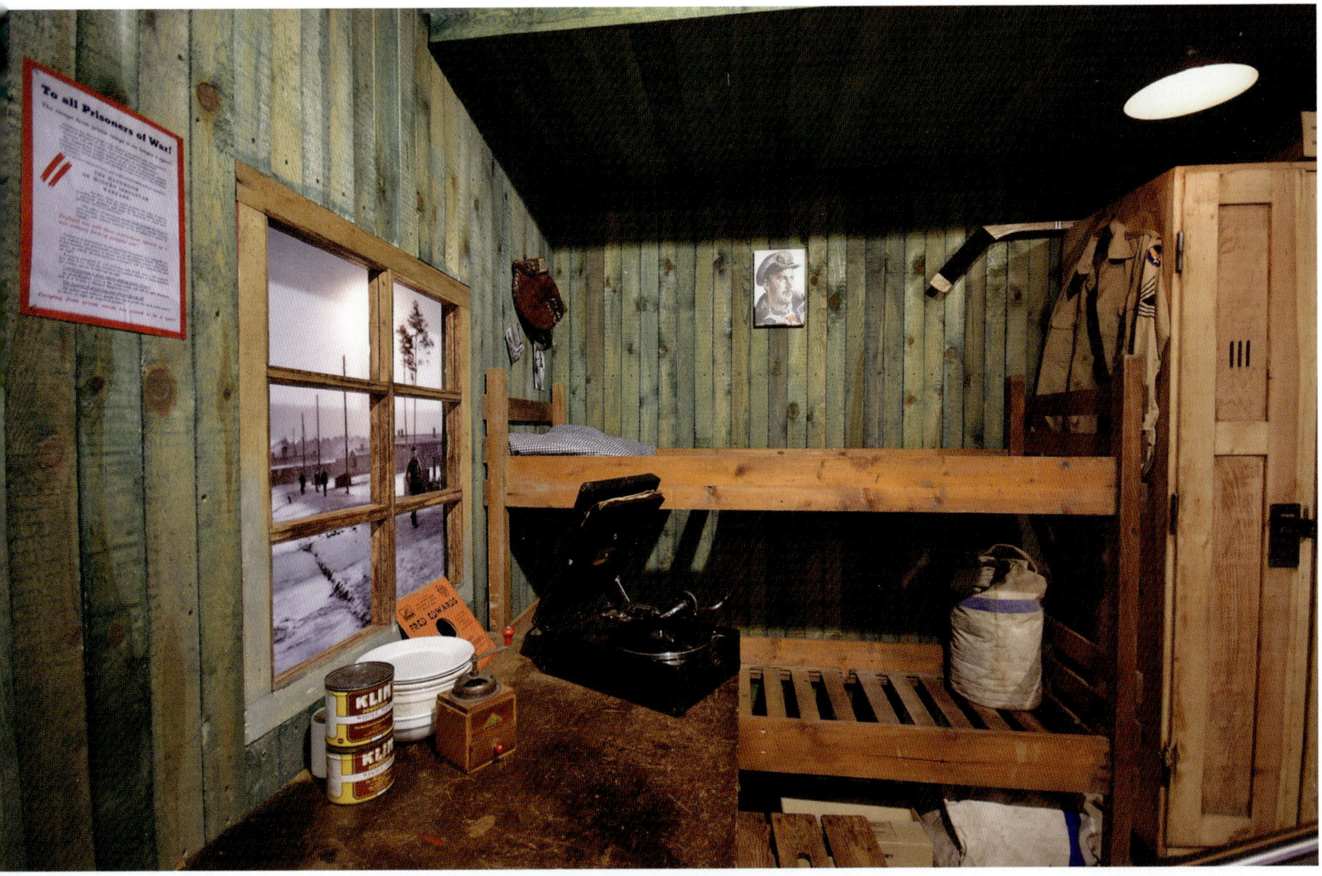

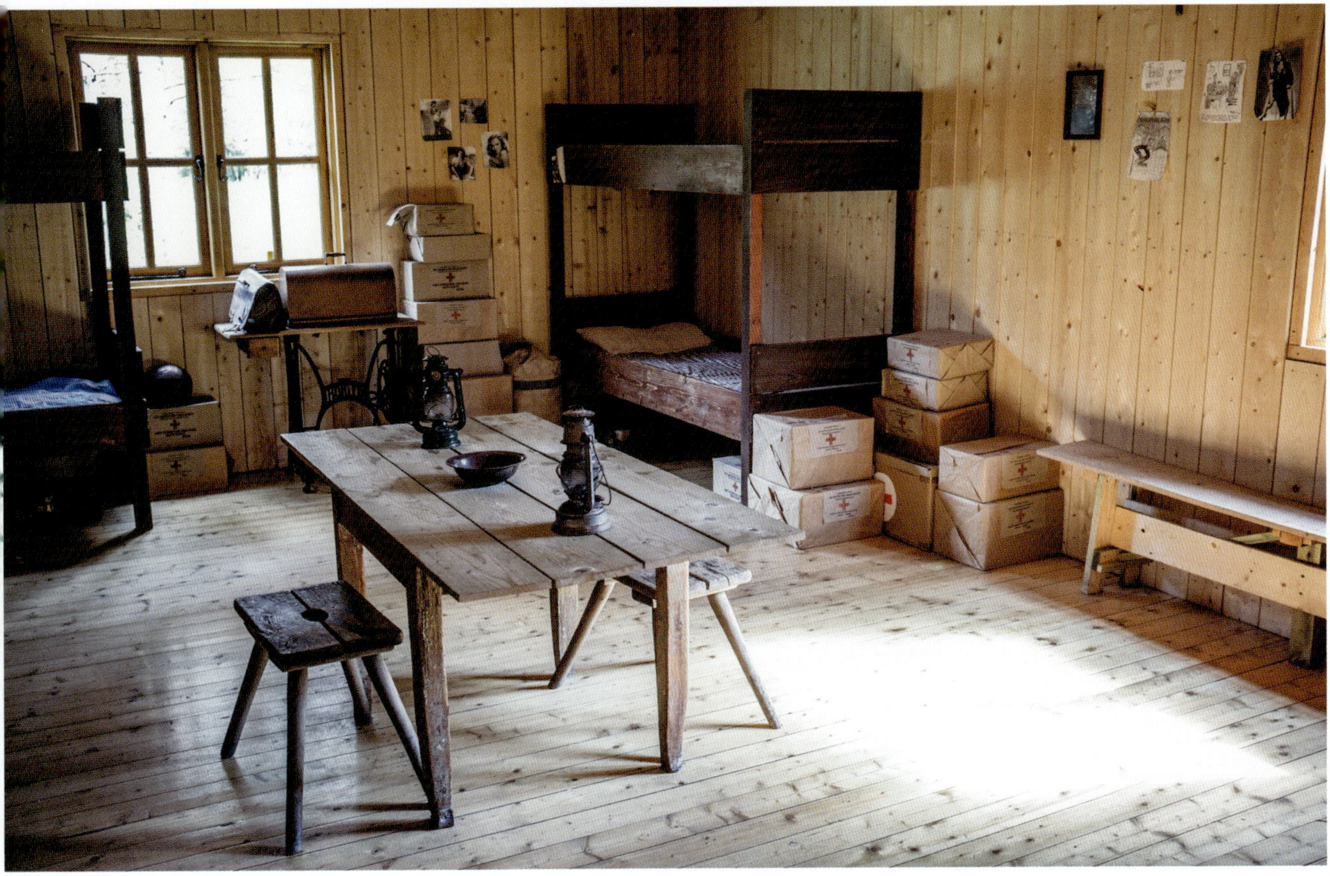

A typical hut stove. It was under one of these that the Great Escape tunnel Harry was started. (*Luka Cyprian*)

Model of Stalag Luft III's North Compound. (*POW Camps Museum*)

A close-up of the same model that was used to film *The Great Escape*. (*Luka Cyprian*)

A wartime map of the German railway system.

(**Above**) Cutlery recovered from the site of Stalag Luft III. The prisoners were issued with spoons and forks on arrival, but if they lost them they had to pay for replacements. (**Below**) Scorched pages of recovered documents and books. *(Luka Cyprian)*

The fifty urns of those murdered after the Great Escape were transferred to the British military cemetery at Poznań after 1945. Seen here are the graves (*left to right*) of Flight Lieutenant Gordon Brettell, Squadron Leader Roger Bushell and Squadron Leader James Catanach. (*Marek Lazarz/POW Camps Museum, Żagań, Poland*)

The memorial to all the POWs who died at Stalag Luft III. In the background is the memorial to the fifty officers murdered after the Great Escape. (*USAFA, SMS 329*)